THE FAMILY BED

AN AGE OLD CONCEPT IN CHILDREARING

by

Tine Thevenin

Foreword by Niles Newton, Ph.D.

Introduction by Herbert Ratner, M.D.

Preface by Marian Tompson, President
La Leche League International

Library of Congress Catalog Card Number: 75-36968
Thevenin, Tine E.
THE FAMILY BED: An Age Old Concept in Childrearing
Minneapolis, Minnesota
January, 1976

ISBN-0-960-2010-1-7

For the blind or physically handicapped: *Loan* copies in cassette or reel-to-reel are available from ILLI Blind Service, 9616 Minneapolis Avenue, Franklin Park, IL 60131

Printed in the United States of America

First Edtion, May, 1976
    First Printing, 2000, May, 1976
    Second Printing, 2000, September, 1976
    Third Printing, 3000, November, 1976
    Fourth Printing, 3000, January, 1977

Second Edition (new cover and expanded) June, 1977
    Fifth Printing, 5000, June, 1977
    Sixth Printing, 5000, March, 1978
    Seventh Printing, 6000, November, 1978
    Eighth Printing, 6000, December, 1979
    Ninth Printing, 6000, December, 1980

                        Tine Thevenin
                        P.O. Box 16004
                        Minneapolis, MN
                        55416

This is an age when men value organizations more than their members. When we force children to conform to our convenience, our schedules, our boundaries, and our locked doors, we show them that we value the system more than we value them.

Dr. James Clark Moloney

DEDICATION

We must continue to search for better ways of living, for if we stop, and accept the present as final and authoritative, we shall no longer grow and progress.

For answers to questions which this search evokes, I always ask myself, how does nature intend for it to be? How far have we become diverted from nature?

I am a young mother living in a society which discourages and belittles these questions. And yet I feel I must try to follow those feelings of motherhood which nature bestowed on me when I gave birth to our children.

I have hope for the future because there is now a growing number of persons who encourage childrearing with love and human understanding, rather than with a schedule in one hand and a clock in the other.

The need people have for one another is not active only during the day, or at pre-determined hours. This need is continuous from the moment of conception, and throughout life, even though it may vary in intensity.

Perhaps the past generations have seen the depth of human misunderstanding. I am hopeful.

It is my wish that this book will be a contribution in the search for a better world, a future which lies in the hands of the children.

I have thus dedicated this book to Yvonne and Michelle, our two beautiful children, with whom my husband and I share our table, our bed, our house, and our life.

T.T.

ACKNOWLEDGEMENT

I wish here to acknowledge the following persons with my deeply felt gratitude. They are listed in the chronological order in which they contributed their services during the course of my writing this book.

Francis, my husband, for making shorter sentences out of my sometimes unbelievably long and complicated ones.

Helen Wessel, for giving me the first suggestion to make a book out of my original ninety page research report; for answering my many questions, and for being the first one to truly make me feel elated when she said, "I could hardly put the manuscript down!"

Lynn Moen, for suggesting the first part of the title.

Niles Newton, for her true interest, her many extremely helpful suggestions and materials, and her encouraging statement, "A book such as this is much needed in our society."

Robert Peters, for designing the book cover.

Hazel Turner, for doing much of the editing of the final copy.

Melanie Kandler for typing the final copy.

I also wish to thank Barbara Wandrei, Robert Genovese, Reynold Mattson, Lucile Cutler, the LLLI Founding Mothers, and also all the parents who participated in the questionnaires.

CONTENTS

DEDICATION vii

ACKNOWLEDGEMENT ix

FOREWORD by Niles Newton, PhD xiii

INTRODUCTION by Herbert Ratner, M.D. xv

PREFACE by Marian Tompson, LLLI President xix

AN OVERSIGHT IN OUR CULTURE 1

THE SOURCES 5

PARENTS FEEL IT WAS MEANT TO BE 9
    Parents' experiences; Positive reasons; We mature; Why it was
    meant to be? Parents tell their story.

WHY SOME PARENTS HESITATE 31
    Nature vs. custom; Negative advice; Drugs for sleep; Parents
    hesitate; Sudden infant death syndrome.

THE IMPORTANCE OF SLEEPING TOGETHER 47
    Importance of love; Importance of touch; The transition phase;
    Bad dreams; Fear; The mind perceives while asleep; A need to
    be understood.

NEED vs. HABIT 61

BRIEF HISTORY OF CHILDHOOD AND FAMILY SLEEPING
CUSTOMS 65
    Medieval to 1700; The change begins: 1700-1800; Bundling;
    The big change: 1800-1900; 1900: The scientific age; The
    return.

SOME ANTHROPOLOGICAL OBSERVATIONS 79

THE INFANT 85
    A hospital birth; Home birth; How baby relaxes; Crying;
    Solutions to crying; Mother and baby may dream in unison;
    Child's sleeping position; Baby awake at night; When will my
    baby sleep through the night?; Breastfeeding while lying down;
    Sleeping arrangements; Conclusion.

THE CHILD PAST INFANCY **111**
Bedtime rituals; Bedtime with Michael; Fear of dark; Fear in falling asleep; When father is away; The older child joins the family bed; The child too old to join the family bed; Dinner guests; Baby who refuses parents' bed; When parent or child is ill; Conclusion.

SIBLINGS **127**

MARITAL RELATIONS **131**
Cross-cultural observations; Historical observations; Private conversations; Marital relations; Natural family planning; Interruptus.

THE ADOPTED CHILD **141**
A mother's testimony; Stepparent.

HOSPITALIZATION OF A MEMBER OF THE FAMILY ... **145**
The child; Mother.

NIGHTTIME IS FOR SLEEPING! **149**
Guiding the child.

CONCLUSION **153**

EPILOGUE by Helen Wessel **159**

APPENDIX—Two Questionnaires **161**

REACTIONS TO THE BOOK **169**

ABOUT THE AUTHOR **175**

RECOMMENDED READING LIST **177**

TABLE OF REFERENCE **179**

BIBLIOGRAPHY **191**

FOREWORD

The easiest place to breastfeed a baby at night is in the bed lying down next to you. The easiest thing to do while nursing this way is to go to sleep while the baby sucks. This gives you much needed rest for the next day. I discovered the advantages of sleep-feeding with my first baby, Willow, and happily fed all four of my children in this simple same manner. Thus, I became one of the millions of mothers all over the world who for thousands of years have followed this biologically based pattern.

You will find many recent "authorities" who can cite theories why sleeping with a baby is "psychologically harmful." Usually they are males or other people who have not had personal experience breastfeeding and caring continuously for a baby throughout the night.

It is interesting how authorities' opinions change with time. A hundred years ago, Dr. Pye Henry Chavasse, the Dr. Spock of his day, wrote in answer to the questions "Ought a babe to lie alone from the first?" The answer was "Certainly not. . .He requires the warmth of another person's body."

The beauty of this book is that it is written by an experienced mother with all the special sensitivity to the issues involved that personal experience gives. Although I do not agree in all instances with the author's interpretation of her sources, I am nevertheless delighted that my own young grandchildren are having the comfort of cuddling their parents in bed and that my daughters and sons-in-law are having easier nights because of it.

The taboo on tenderness that we see so often in the Western world does not have to be followed by individual families. Touching and cuddling can be one of the foundations of a warm family life. This does not have to be limited to the daytime hours.

Niles Newton, Ph.D.
Professor, Division of Psychology
Department of Psychiatry
Northwestern University Medical School
Chicago, Illinois 60611

INTRODUCTION

Were modern society thriving with high level wellness at all ages and stages of life, physicians and others interested in childrearing would have a right to dismiss a book promoting the old-fashioned notion that the parental bed be converted into a family bed. With modern society, however, suffering from a marked dysfunctioning and harboring doubts that there will be a viable society to turn over to the next generation, we can afford to be open minded about a practice which purports to contribute to the emotional security of a human being.

The indices of a sick society—alienation and psychiatric illness, suicide attempts and suicide, alcoholism and drug misuse, infidelity and divorce, pornography and perversion, sexual restlessness and impotency, juvenile delinquency, child abuse and violent crime—have been steadily rising since World War I. Psychiatry, for the most part, has responded remedially and ineffectively: at the technologic level with shock therapy, frontal lobotomies and psychopharmaceuticals (billions of dollars are now spent on tranquilizers); at the psychologic level with an unawareness or insensitivity to nurturent needs and with a permissiveness which, severed from controlling social norms, reflects an excessive counter-reaction to a preceding Victorian age.

Unfortunately, today's mental health movement is a movement primarily concerned with the management of mental illness, not with the promotion of mental health, the latter being hardly more than a platitudinous window-dressing. Physicians in general, and psychiatrists in particular, (neither of whom are especially competent in their own family life or even partially immune from personal psychiatric problems), preoccupied with patient problems and lulled by the blandishments of drug companies and the ready promises of the prescription pad, fail to reflect on and explore the true nature of a mental health movement—one directed to the preservation, promotion and perfection of the initial mental health with which man is endowed at birth.

For though nature turns over to us more than three million babies a year, virtually all of whom are psychologically healthy, the fact is that the majority of them, despite continuing medical attendance (or because of it), grow up emotionally insecure, and one out of ten newborns enters a mental institution sometime in the course of his or her lifetime. Now, especially that it is becoming virtually impossible to supply enough psychiatrists, psychiatric social workers, nurses, and psychiatric facilities to handle the mounting number of patients needing help, it would seem that society should turn its attention to the earlier years to see when and how things went wrong. It is perhaps our only hope for stemming the tide of psychiatrically crippled human beings.

What we must be mindful of if we have any respect for nature is that she has accumulated a built-in wisdom born of a vast clinical experience over millions of years, out of which a reciprocal fitness between the living thing and its environment has evolved. In mammalia this is found particularly in the intimate relationship of mother and young. The mother is nature's 'prepared environment' for the newborn! We cannot afford to ignore this wisdom. Literally this is what the natural sciences are about: to discover the wisdom of nature: that is, the laws, nuances and subtleties of nature which enabled our species to survive and prosper. In the meantime, to bridge the gap between what we already know (or think we know) and what we have yet to learn—what is yet to be discovered by the activities of countless researchers in thousands of laboratories—the prudent and sagacious man must seek his cues and clues and norms from the operations of nature. Here we must remember that medicine, in its broadest sense, is a normative art.

The fatal mistake we have made in medicine, not only in psychiatry but even more so in pediatrics and obstetrics, was to introduce practices which deviated from normal physiologic and psychologic processes without first firmly researching the full implications and wisdom of man-imposed changes. This is best exemplified by the ignorance inherent in the ready substitution of bottle feeding for breastfeeding as if, to recall Oliver Wendell Holmes, the two hemispheres of the contemporary pediatrician's brain is superior to a pair of mammary glands in the art of compounding a nutritive fluid for infants. We forget that the root of the word *physician* is *phusis* which means nature, and that medicine is a cooperative art because it cooperates with the active mechanisms of nature and the goal of nature which it shares. (The same mistake is also seen by our having made the drugged and operative hospital delivery the prevalent as opposed to the natural delivery.)

The fitness of the environment for the living, whose fitness is reciprocal to the environment, is not only a matter of the physical, such as water, oxygen, nitrogen, carbon and trace minerals, but also of the psychologic, as seen by the maternal and parental environment without which the young of mammalia cannot survive or emotionally mature. Here it must be stressed that it is the family, not the individual, which is the proper unit of care, because the family, especially as it concerns the psyche, is the maker or breaker of health.

The fact that modern medicine and technology, despite its many brilliant accomplishments, has not given society high, or even low, level wellness (nor has the huge amount of money we have expended, as if health were a commodity that could be bought in the market place (*Child & Family*. 7:73-4, 1968) nor even slowed up the prevailing malaise that is enveloping our country should make us reconsider our problem and its solution.

Accordingly, it is incumbent upon the reader, particularly those who are professionals in the medical and behavioral sciences, to approach *The Family Bed* with an open mind. It cogently brings to life the manner in which a family functions or may function in attaining its purpose—the giving of mature adults to society at large. Enough studies now exist to document with finality that the first years of life are vital if not crucial to adult maturity; that the indices of a sick society are symptomatic manifestations in later life of insecurities generated in earlier years. Even academia—the Harvard studies under Dr. Burton White—reaffirm the importance of full-time attention of a mother (or a mother substitute) to the dependent child in his or her first two or three years of life for the child's optimal emotional development. The time is long overdue for parents, physicians, social agencies and government experts to realize that they have been working at the wrong end of the age scale in seeking basic solutions. We must recognize that the dysfunctioning family should be corrected and helped to function properly in its work as the prime health maker for society.

The Family Bed is a case in point. The author's thesis is that there is something natural, right and salutary in the desire of young children to convert the parental bed into a family bed. The exposition of her thesis is substantial. In fact, it is as if Maria Montessori whispered in her ear, "If you want to understand the needs of children, observe and study the child." That very young children, always and everywhere—in contrast to older children—prefer the family bed to their own bed or their own room communicates a convincing message. Since man is not only a social animal but a gregarious animal as well, the ramifications of interfering with such a universal, inborn natural inclination may be extensive.

One of the great strengths of *The Family Bed* stems from the author's recognition of the experience and convictions of mothers who accept rather than reject motherhood as a vocation and who make a point of trying to enrich their vocation by participating in mothering organizations such as La Leche League International. Many of these mothers have large families, mothers whom Sir James Spence characterized as really good at motherhood. (The Purpose of the Family. *Child and Family.* 7:328. 1968) Such mothers, practitioners as opposed to theorists, are the real experts. They contrast to the Spocks and Salks, who, when they are right, are simply echoes of what the good mother has learned by being attentive and responsive to the voice of nature. Profundity characterizes the simple conclusion of a mother that "Babies wants and needs are one and the same thing"; or of another, "Society has taken away the right of a baby to be dependent upon his mother."

The Family Bed is most readable. It will bring joy and support to parents who refuse to reject the silent (and sometimes not so silent) importunings of their children and who refuse to banish them to isolated, solitary outposts. It will help other parents take a second look at what parenthood is all about. Parents tell me that the best advice I gave them as young couples entering marriage and parenthood was first, to invest in a king-size bed, and second, to never forget that the fastest road to furthering independence in their children is total attention to the needs of their children in their dependent years.

Herbert Ratner, M.D., Editor
Child & Family Quarterly

PREFACE

This is an important book and an unusual one. It explores the pros and cons, the joys and irritations occuring when children sleep with their parents. And at the same time hopefully relieves unnecessary anxieties suffered by parents pledged to take their children into their hearts—but never into their beds.

If you've allowed your little one to sleep with you on occasion but kept it a family secret, this is the book for you. If you've wondered what happens when families fly in the face of all that's "decent" while attempting to meet needs of their children in this way, read on. And if the whole idea makes you a bit uneasy well, keep an open mind. After all you might be reacting rather normally as a citizen of this brave new world where even breastfeeding is sometimes considered unusual.

The loving testimonies of those who've tried it and their good feelings about their families add the kind of inspiration we all can use. In her book Tine Thevenin presents an old-fashioned philosophy of parenting which I believe deserves much thoughtful consideration today.

Marian Tompson, President
La Leche League International

AN OVERSIGHT OF OUR CULTURE

Our days, our deeds, all we achieve or are,
Lie folded in our infancy.
                    —John T. Trowbridge

Most of us have read or heard sometime, somewhere what an "authority" advises on children sleeping with their parents or with other siblings. Although the opinions on this subject are quite controversial, the practice is usually discouraged.

One may pick up many a book on childrearing and read that bad sleeping habits in a child are formed when mother hears her baby whimper and "rushes" in to see if everything is all right. The child will wake up more frequently, these books tell us, just to get his mother near him.

A mother is ridiculed for wanting to pick up her crying baby. Yet, this response to a call, the concern for her offspring, is an action which comes from the very depth of her motherhood.

The child is scolded for reaching out to his parent during a time of need. He is to be told "lovingly" but firmly that nighttime is not a time for his parents' love and attention.

These are the books that strongly advise parents against taking their children to bed with them, whether in time of stress or as a matter of course. The parent is neither allowed nor encouraged to place trust and value in his own parental emotions, but instead becomes the innocent victim of old prejudices that linger on. If he does not follow the advice, then he must rely on his own wandering common sense, or be harrassed by wondering what to do. Our society

1

proclaims co-family sleeping as taboo. It also gives us no satisfactory answers to bed and nighttime problems with children.

The parental instinct concerning an offspring is not to be underestimated, although for many years this seemed to be the case. But times are changing. In a newspaper article of January, 1974, Dr. Spock is quoted as saying he admits parents of this country have been persuaded that only trained persons know how children should be reared. This, he continues, has resulted in a lack of self assurance on the part of the parents. He goes so far as to call it a "cruel deprivation" that has been imposed on mothers and fathers.

In 1974, another article appeared in a publication entitled "Why Some Babies Don't Sleep." (*English Journal*. "New Society"). The authors of this article found that the most common problem causing parents' concern was the child's waking at night. In their comments on the result of their research they wrote that some of the advice which frequently comes from health visitors, welfare clinics and general practitioners is not always very helpful and may actually have little real experience behind it. The minimum research, they report, which is done on this problem compared with matters concerning hospital care of sick babies, is, as a matter of fact, striking. "What has emerged from the research," they continue, "has not filtered through very effectively to those who need it."

What do parents have to say on this subject? A young mother wrote, "I deeply feel that our baby should be with us during the night. However, she has a bedroom of her own. Why? I do not know. I wish it could be different. We frequently have such difficulty in getting her to sleep without crying. I wish I knew what to do."

I was this mother, writing about our first child when she was nine months old. As a new parent it never occurred to me then to take her into bed with my husband and me.

By the time our second child was born, we had talked about this subject with various people. To our great surprise, we found many who "confessed" to taking their children into bed with them. They did so usually because of a child's sleeping problem or because it seemed to result in a happier family.

Many of these parents tended to express a belief in other more natural approaches to childrearing; e.g. natural childbirth, breastfeeding, natural family planning. They felt that co-family sleeping, either children with their parents or siblings with siblings, fit logically in the philosophy of the natural approach.

This book brings to light the experiences and opinions of those parents who have their children sleep with them. It also presents additional supportive medical, historical and cultural data. Co-family sleeping is advocated here as a way to solve bed and nighttime problems with children, create a closer bond within the family, and give children a greater sense of security. It supports a concept in child-rearing which has been practiced throughout the ages, throughout the world.

" IT'S EASY FOR YOU TO SAY, 'DON'T BE AFRAID OF THE DARK'...
...YOU GOT SOMEBODY TO SLEEP WITH!"

"Dennis the Menace" © by Field Newspaper Synd. T.M.®

THE SOURCES

Happiness is the atmosphere in which
all good affections grow.
　　　　　　　　　　—Thomas Bray

The content of this book is based on telephone conversations, two questionnaires, correspondence, and exhaustive library research. There were ninety-five returns on the first questionnaire, and forty-seven returns on the second.

The purpose of the two questionnaires was to find answers to questions such as:

1. Why do parents have their children sleep with them?
2. Does it seem advantageous to have siblings sleep together?
3. When do children begin sleeping away from the parental bed?
4. What about sexual relations?
5. What solutions have parents found to accommodate more people in their beds?
6. What is the opinion of the parents?

I place much value in the content of the returns of these questionnaires.* We have read and heard opinions on this subject from doctors and psychiatrists. These persons, by nature of their profession, are often associated primarily with abnormal, maladjusted

---

*I have incorporated portions of these returns throughout the book. See also appendix.

5

cases, cases which were brought to them because they needed professional attention. Nowhere do we read what a normal, relatively well-adjusted family does, how its members feel about sleeping together, and what experiences they have had.

By necessity, I have had to rely on the members of La Leche League. They, as a group, are the ones most likely to take their children into bed with them. La Leche League is an organization which encourages breastfeeding, and has been the inspiration to many a mother to follow and uphold her inner convictions concerning motherhood.

According to a study by Dr. Niles Newton in which the behavior of nursing and non-nursing mothers was compared, the mothers differed significantly in their willingness to share a bed with their babies. The women who breastfed their children, says Newton, appear less concerned with current cultural disapproval of bedsharing.[1]

A great majority of successful breastfeeding mothers take their babies to bed with them. However, as comparatively few mothers breastfeed in our culture, it is no wonder that family bed sharing is not the norm. Many parents have never even heard of it, let alone considered it. In cultures in which breastfeeding is the norm, bed sharing is frequently as common as the sharing of the family dinner table is in our own culture.

Many parents replied that La Leche League specifically helped them in realizing the benefits of having their young children sleeping with them. They have relied heavily on its support. I, too, feel that it is greatly through this organization that my husband and I have been able to venture out and discover the warm beauty of having our children sleep with us.*

I emphasize that this book is not one of statistics, nor am I defending the main idea. My object is to give insight, encouragement and reason for co-family sleeping.

---

*A note may be made of the fact that no specific age of the child has been mentioned. He may be referred to as baby, or young child, or child. This has been done to alleviate the strong influence the mention of the age and the child's expected accomplishments may have on parents. For example, if we read that children between one and two years of age usually sleep twelve to fourteen hours, we sometimes tend to forget the word "usually."

Among children who are accustomed to sleeping with someone from birth on, there seems to be a natural graduation from needing to sleep in the parental bed per se to sleeping with other siblings. This book's emphasis is on the young child. It is to be understood, therefore, that when I speak of sleeping together, i.e. co-family sleeping, the implication is sleeping with whomsoever he chooses according to his emotional development. Thus some children are ready to leave the family bed at age two, yet others may not be ready till a much later age.

Twenty years ago, when prepared or natural childbirth was a new thought, little information was available on the subject. Many people, doctors and laymen alike, scoffed at the idea. Today, because the medical profession and mothers have found it so right for the mother to be awake and aware during her labor and birth, prepared childbirth is no longer a novelty. It is becoming accepted, and proving to be highly beneficial and effective.

Likewise, breastfeeding is slowly making its re-entry. There is now scientific proof that nursing at the breast is superior to any other infant feeding method. During the last fifteen to twenty years an increasing number of publications on the great advantages of breastfeeding have been appearing on the market.

So, also, co-family sleeping is a new thought—though new mostly since the last century. Before this natural behavior will again become accepted, its importance and benefits too will have to be proven scientifically. Thirty years ago it might have been difficult to obtain sufficient convincing evidence. Thirty years ago this book might have had little support. Today a growing amount of research on the negative results of separation of a mother and her child is becoming available and accepted. Bowlby's book *Separation*, volume two of *Attachment and Loss*, goes into the greatest detail describing the effects on a child when he is prematurely separated from his mother. The author, who is a world authority on maternal attachment and deprivation, discusses the possible psychopathic results from such separation. Interestingly enough, Bowlby makes no mention of the generally widely accepted separation during the nighttime sleeping which takes place in the majority of families in the Western world today. And he barely discusses a child's life from birth to six months. However, his presentation is so well documented, that an inference could be drawn that the routine nocturnal separation and isolation from birth on can also have a possible negative effect on the child in one form or another. Science is now "proving" that which many a mother's heart has known for millennia, "My child needs me."

PARENTS FEEL IT WAS MEANT TO BE

The home we first knew on this beautiful earth,
The friends of our childhood, the place of our birth,
In the hearts' inner chamber sung always will be,
As the shell ever sings of its home in the sea.
  —*Francis Dana Gage, "Home."*

It is quiet. It is dark. It is night. Somewhere a baby whimpers. His mother stirs and pulls her infant toward her. He nuzzles for her breast. He begins to nurse and both Babe and Mom fall back to sleep. Somewhere in his dream Papa knows all is well. All are asleep.

Somewhere a toddler awakens, and sleepily speaks, "Mama?" Mama stirs in her sleep, she reaches over and takes the child's hand in her hand. They both fall back to sleep. Papa's dreams were not even interrupted. All is well. All are asleep.

Whether it be on a Japanese "futon," or under an arctic caribou skin, on the bare African ground, in a large four poster bed, or in a double-twin size bed, whether they be poor or rich, large or small, many families all over the world sleep together, and have done so since the beginning of mankind.

Separate sleeping is mainly a social custom; and, as is true of social customs, they change with the times. The Western world has seen a hundred years or so in which separate sleeping has been strongly advocated; so strongly as a matter of fact that many parents feel guilty in taking their children to bed with them. However, the time has now come in which parents are not necessarily satisfied

9

with doing things the way their parents did them. They are questioning doing "as they are told."

Modern parents are seeking fulfillment which they perhaps instinctively feel has been lacking. A mother, pregnant for the second time, hesitantly agrees to attend prepared childbirth classes. Her first birth, an experience in which she was unable to participate as fully as possible, has left her with vague, dissatisfied memories. The second birth is beautiful. She has prepared herself and is awake and aware when her child is born. A bottlefeeding mother decides to breastfeed. . .after all, it was meant to be. What a glorious experience! How wonderful this closeness. "No," she says, "I'll not let you be taken away from me and put into another bed, in another room. We belong together." Mother and baby nestle together in bed. Father puts his protective arm around the two. Then they fall asleep. It, too, was meant to be.

Perhaps to those who have never experienced sleeping peacefully with their own children this may all sound rather idealistic. However, it is not so, as parents will continually relate throughout this book.

It is not my intention to compare the pros and cons on the experiences of co-family sleeping. Rather, let us read why many parents have a positive attitude toward sleeping together.

PARENTS' EXPERIENCES

There are parents who have never read much about childrearing They just do what comes naturally. "We allowed our child to sleep with us because we just felt it was the easiest, most natural thing to do," a young couple wrote. "In fact, we had never even thought about it as being different until we mentioned it to other people."

In trying to understand their children's needs it has helped parents to recall their own childhood when they would seek refuge in their parents' bed during stressful times. It felt so safe and reassuring.

Even lying down with them till they fall asleep is not enough for some children. Parents remember sadly not being allowed in their parents' bed. "I was never allowed in my parents' bed," writes a young mother. "I can remember many nights feeling tremendously frightened and lonely, but knowing that I really shouldn't go and wake them. Sometimes my mother or father would come into my room and lie down with me, but it was just not the same. All the while I knew that they'd leave as soon as I had fallen asleep. I never want our children to feel unwelcome."

But those parents who did experience family sleeping in their young years remember it fondly. "I slept with my parents off and on until I was eight years old. So did my brother. My mother now sleeps with her grandchildren on every occasion she has. She says it brings back memories of the time when we were little. We are still a closeknit and loving family. P.S. If a Mom or Dad were not available to climb into bed with, a brother, aunt or grandparent would always oblige willingly."

Most parents wrote that with their firstborn they started the family sleeping arrangement in the conventional way; separate bedrooms for the child and no permission for him to come into bed with them. But slowly, with each additional child, they changed their views and began favoring co-family sleeping.

"With our first child I was much more concerned with 'high' childrearing ideals," a mother of two children wrote to me. "We became more relaxed with our second one. The benefits showed on the first child also."

One mother found it impossible, with her fifth child, to get in and out of the bed in order to minister to him, and still assure herself of the proper rest. When the infant was a few weeks old, mother was so exhausted she took baby to bed with her. They stayed there will morning. She found that her infant slept longer and better and she could doze even while breastfeeding him. The arrangement was so satisfactory that it became permanent for the next three years. The other children, too, occasionally joined them in bed. She commented, "I could now cope better with being a wife and mother. As a result my husband was also happier."

Parents found that children awakened in a much more pleasant mood than when they had slept alone in their own bed. "They wake up with a smile," wrote a mother. "We feel that children were meant to sleep with their parents."

Several parents expressed the opinion that since their family began to sleep together, its members were more relaxed, touched one another more, and felt closer to each other. One mother, realizing the importance of touch, wrote, "Our family does not 'touch' physically as much as I would like. Night contact is one way of

11

making up for this."

While some mothers feel they sleep less when their child is with them, others experience just the opposite. "I simply feel more comfortable, sleep longer, more deeply, and am more relaxed when my children are next to me."

POSITIVE REASONS

The majority of reasons which parents gave for not allowing their children to sleep with them were mainly parent-oriented ones (see section on "The Importance of Sleeping Together"). Those who were in favor, however, gave both parent- ("It was easier. We enjoy it."), as well as child-oriented reasons ("Because my child seemed to need it.").

Following is a list of reasons parents gave as to why they had their children sleep with them.

- Incidence of night problems, teething, bad dreams. (Bad dreams incidentally were mentioned very frequently.)
- We feel baby needs 24-hour continuous closeness with mother.
- When we are in strange surroundings, it acts as a form of security.
- To relax the child and get him off to sleep.
- From exhaustion—being up at night.
- Too cold to get up at night to tend to baby.
- We enjoyed the closeness, and like snuggling with them.
- When we feel especially close to him.
- It just happened over the years.
- Due to limited amount of heat during the night.
- Because of emotional benefits.
- As a method of childspacing. Since baby could nurse freely at night, it thus helped to suppress ovulation. (See Bibliography; Kippley, John and Sheila.)
- This way we were always aware of his well-being.
- We truly had the feeling that he belonged to us, that we were all one big family.
- Husband thought the baby looked lonely.
- It fulfills my protective and mothering instinct.
- It is easier when I (mother) am ill.

12

- It is easier when a child is ill.
- Because husband and children want it.
- Because of memories of my own childhood.
- We enjoy the quiet time together with one or more children.
- At 2 a.m. I'm too tired to object.
- Lack of sleeping places.
- It is the easiest way to keep the children quiet and get them off to sleep.

So contrary to those who bemoan not having enough room to stretch out when children are in their bed, some parents take it all in stride. They emphasize the positive qualities. "I often think as I lie 'squished' between my dear husband on one side and our two or four year old on the other, 'I am such a lucky woman to be so close to the people I love so very much.' "

Parents glow with warmth and pride when they speak of their experiences. "One of my most treasured memories is lying in bed with my husband and our newborn son between us. I felt then more complete, fulfilled and ecstatic than ever before."

The family that is accustomed to sleeping together finds it no problem at all when it goes out camping, stays overnight at a relative's home, or for some reason has to bundle together for lack of space or beds.

One mother wrote, "We enjoy having our friends stay overnight. There is no fuss or worry about where baby sleeps. Of course he sleeps with Mom and Dad. There is no need for a crib or playpen, swing or infant seat, or any of the other gadgets which serve as a mother substitute. If people only knew how simple mothering can be. One mother, one baby, one Dad, maybe a baby carrier, some nice warm convenient breast milk, a dry diaper, and life is easy and relaxed. I love to be cuddly and warm. Don't you? Why not the rest of the family enjoy this wonderful closeness?"

The parental bed seems to be a focal point for activities other than sleeping. Parents have noticed that their children like to read, look out of the window, play games or just lounge on their bed. Pre-schoolers take naps more easily, and one mother even felt that sick children become well more quickly! It is a beautiful cure-all.

I have not had any correspondence with handicapped mothers. I would assume, however, that they also may benefit greatly from having children, especially very small children, sleep with them. In the book *In This Sign* by Joanne Greenberg, the young mother Janice slept with her hand on her newborn baby. Janice is a deaf-mute mother. She would be awakened when she felt her baby begin to cry.

The news media, too, are bringing the idea of children in the parental bed more into the open. A diaper advertisement shows a picture of a baby sleeping with Mother. A promotion for cozy, warm blankets shows a whole family reading a book in bed before getting up in the morning.

And in one newspaper a letter was printed by a mother who, by her own explanation, wished to thank all the mothers in Minnesota who, by their example, had indirectly encouraged her to have her children sleep in the family bed. She felt that society went wrong with its sterile customs of assigning each child a separate bedroom or bed. As so many parents, she also found that their youngest child, who slept with his parents until he chose to sleep with his siblings, turned out to be a most loving and considerate youngster. "The bigger the bed, the better," she writes. Many other young families have a "family bed" now, she continues. "After all," she ends her letter, "who of us doesn't have wonderful memories of crawling into our own parents' bed?"

WE MATURE

One of the most laudable aspects of a person's childrearing ways is his ability to place his highest value in his child rather than in things. This form of maturity takes time, however, and not infrequently have several children entered the family before a parent has grown into this realization. It takes time and growing along with the children to be able to truly balance the influence of clocks, social opinions, and material objects with the needs of our children. We become more relaxed about certain aspects of childrearing and family living. We realize that book theories cannot usually be applied verbatim to our highly individual children. As we look back we sigh and say, "If I could do it over again...." So it is with sleeping arrangements. Many of the returns stated wishfully that it would be different if it could be done all over again.

"I wish," writes one parent, "we could have had a king-size bed when we were first married. It would have helped a lot. If I could do it all over again, I'd like to have two or three mattresses on the

14

floor so everyone could sleep together until the children wanted to have their own room or bed. I'm sure that before too long some of our children will want privacy, but until that time I want them to feel welcome in our bed."

And another parent admits: "We changed the sleeping arrangements from separate to all together with our third and fourth children. We grew up, matured, and changed our values from things to people."

Other parents mentioned how they matured in becoming less self-centered, self-interested. A mother told me, "I used to tell my little two year old, 'I need my sleep too. You are in the way when you sleep with me.' Now, two children later, I realize that once I shifted the interest in myself to my children, many of the inconveniences which irritated me and were so mammoth have diminished in importance."

Quite a few parents have referred to themselves as being "dumb," "stupid," "immature," or "too self-centered," in refusing their first few children their bed. Once they had allowed the children with them they felt matured, fulfilled, wise, more understanding of the needs of others.

I consider it to be noteworthy that I have found no indications of families who have reversed their opinions and sleeping habits from co-family sleeping on a regular basis to separate sleeping. When co-family sleeping was forced, such as on a vacation trip, then yes, some parents could not wait to sleep by themselves again. But when it involved a maturing and growing understanding of the children's needs, then the change to co-family sleeping seemed also to grow in acceptance.

WHY IT WAS MEANT TO BE

From these growing years what wonderful memories we will have to treasure for the rest of our lives. Anyone who has ever awakened in the morning to find his little child curled up against him, so peacefully sleeping, so utterly trusting, knows what I mean when I say I'm convinced that this must be the right thing to do.

There is nothing more precious, nothing that can compare.

I remember being awakened by my little girl who had not yet weaned. I, however, was not facing her. She was touching my back saying, "Mama!" Then she sat up and peeked over. "There it

15

is!" she exclaimed, delighted. She swung over, nestled against me, and began to nurse contentedly. We both fell asleep again.

We were meant to bring forth children in love and happiness. See your child unhappy and you will be unhappy. See your child full of laughter, and you will be the happiest person. Children love to be with people. Let's make them happy and have them sleep with their parents or brothers and sisters. After all, it really was meant to be this way. How do we know? Ask a happy child who was allowed to sleep with another human being. Ask a happy mother who has experienced the tenderness of her sleeping child snuggled next to her in bed.

PARENTS TELL THEIR STORY

The value of these testimonies is four-fold.

1. It gives the reader a deeper insight into the experiences and opinions of families, most of whom have traveled the road from no-child-in-our-bed to all-are-welcome.

2. It gives insight into the pattern of change. It will be observed that basically the changes came about in much the same way in each family.

3. These are accounts written by *mothers*, not scholars of human behavior. Throughout this book reference is made to scientific resources "proving" or "disproving" a particular human behavior; actions, reactions and feelings. It is interesting to read by what simple thoughts mothers can express feelings about which great scholars write lengthy books. Of course, research sheds much insight and we can learn from its endeavors. But perhaps we should at times be equally concerned about truly listening to expressions of basic maternal and paternal instincts.

4. It gives insight into the fact that the feelings which are aroused by parenting in one mother are basically felt by many mothers.

TESTIMONIES

By Mrs. W. who has six children, ages fourteen months through nineteen years.

The very first time we had a child in our bed was when our first born was big enough to climb out of his crib, at about eighteen months. We were too sleepy that night to be analytical of the child-in-bed-with-parents situation, so we welcomed him, plus a big stuffed animal that came with him. The following day I fixed his crib so he could climb out without possibly getting hurt. He continued to come to our bed from then on. Sometimes he would come for several nights in succession. At other times he would come in just for an occasional night.

Our second child exhibited fear of noises, the wind and the dark. As soon as she could get out of her crib, she too came frequently to our bed when she awakened at night. However, she came less often than our first child because she shared a room with her big brother. This in itself seemed to lessen her fears. Sometimes, instead of coming to us, she crawled into bed with her brother.

Our third and fourth children followed much the same pattern: as soon as they were able, they went leaping over the crib side and into bed with a sibling. These two preferred their siblings' beds to the masterbed. When they outgrew their cribs, we invested in two double beds and put our four children together.

The real rooming-in began with our fifth child. With four other children to care for during the daytime hours, and a job to uphold, it was imperative that mother and father get their sleep at night. After four weeks of being up at all odd hours with my newborn, I discovered that everyone could get a lot more sleep when baby slept with me. Sometimes if baby had a restless night, father resorted to sleeping elsewhere in the house. This is certainly a small inconvenience for the larger gain of everyone's getting necessary rest. The child nursed frequently during the night during his first year and into the second and third years.

When "baby" was three years old, we felt that he should have his own bed for purposes of identity if not for every night occupancy. He liked the idea. I nursed him in the living room or bedroom prior to tucking him in. Having contented himself at the breast, he then went up to bed. Sometimes he chose to sleep with his parents or siblings instead of in his own bed. Whenever Daddy was working nights, this youngest child knew that there was an empty slot next to me and he usually claimed it, although by this time our third and fourth children had become interested in sleeping with us and they asked to

17

take turns.   So our household had a very flexible sleeping arrangement.

Just before the youngest's fourth birthday, we had our sixth child, and for the first time in our childbearing years there was not a crib in the house. It was assumed that baby Raphael would sleep with us until he asked for a bed of his own. Our older children still want to sleep with us sometimes. Perhaps this is mainly because they like to be near the baby. A mattress that we have alongside the bed holds any and all who want to join us. Somehow that mattress came to be called the "clubhouse," which, now that I think of it, is a definition of a place where friends with a common purpose meet and communicate.

During the past year my husband's work has required him to arise at five a.m., so in order not to awaken the sleeping herd, he chooses to sleep in another room on his working nights.

In summary I would describe our sleeping situation as subject to variation. Neither spouse feels threatened by the need of children for their parents during the night. We see nighttime needs to be as important as daytime needs. As our family has grown in size and age, what was once the typical, much talked about connubial chamber, has certainly undergone some changes. These changes, we are convinced, are for the betterment of mankind. Whatever inconveniences or disappointments we might have faced, the end product is completely satisfying.

My answer to that tired old question, how do you have sexual relations with children nearby is, "without fanfare and when it is convenient."   A more serious question might be, do you disturb one another when all sleep so close to each other? My reply is "sometimes, but surely not always." Our sleep is also disturbed by loud neighbors, the telephone, airplanes, sirens, etc. We feel our own children are the least of any disturbances which occur during sleep.

One last parting thought. Last week our nine year old awakened ill and it was decided he should stay home from school for the day. Without any previous comment he left his own bed, brought his get-well equipment with him, and set up shop in his parents' bed. He probably would have recovered in any bed or room in the house. But his choice of quarters for healing purposes was interesting to observe.

By Mrs. O. who has eight children, ages four through eighteen years.

Our first four children were born before we became familiar with La Leche League philosophies. They slept in cribs away from our bedroom.

When La Leche League came into our life, my husband was delighted to hear that it was all right to have the children sleep with us. It was not so with me! I didn't like to sleep like a pretzel. I liked to sleep cuddled next to my husband, without a baby between us. But gradually, as he insisted, I saw the wisdom behind this "new" idea. Our fifth baby loved it, and I discovered a definite new response in this baby that had not been evident in the other four children. I had always wanted to hug and cuddle our babies, but they had squirmed and seemed to be very independent. They did not respond as I thought babies should. But this baby loved to touch, caress, and stroke me, and she loved this in return. An emotional closeness was developing between us which had been missing with the older children.

I watched this new fifth baby in her sleep and observed that she always slept with at least one part of her body touching either me or my husband. If she stirred and lost this contact, she would grope around—still in her sleep—till she touched skin again. She would then relax and lie content. She continued to sleep with us until she was old enough to sleep in the bottom part of a bunk bed.

When Joe, our sixth child, was born he also slept with us. (At age eight, he is still a regular partner in our bed.) Two years after Joe, our seventh child was born. By this time our bed was getting crowded. We bought a king-size bed, thinking this would solve the problem. But it only served as an invitation to more of the youngsters. And now it is common to have two or three of our eight children sleeping with us. The three eldest never do. They were probably too old by the time we opened our bed to the children.

I've tried to analyze why my husband was so eager to have the children sleep with us. He was the seventh child in a family of eight, and he was held a great deal. As a young child he used to crawl in bed with his mother after his Dad went to milk the cows early in the morning. During the early years of our marriage he worked long hours. He missed seeing the children and therefore got into the habit of waking them at eleven p.m. for a short visit.

Now, even though he works from eight a.m. till five p.m., he still remembers those evening hours away from the children, and he tells them before they fall asleep to come into our bed if they wake during the night. Frequently three to five of them will fall asleep in our bed. We carry them into their own beds to make room for us.

I've long since discarded my reluctance to their presence in our bed, and do enjoy their company. The advantages of the real closeness which has developed far outweighs any problems. And we will have precious memories.

By Mrs. P. who has seven children, ages nine through twenty-six years.

We've been married for over twenty-six years. Our firstborn slept in a crib in our room for only three months. He was then moved to his own room. Our next three babies slept in our room in a crib for at least one year. It was always a comfort for the infant and us to be so close. And it was reassuring that we could readily be aware should he have a need for us.

Our children always chose to sleep with at least one other person. We now have five bedrooms, but even with seven children, two rooms are always empty.

We have told our children that any time they are disturbed or frightened during the night, they could come into our bed. This they have always done. And when any one of them was sick or feverish, my husband or I slept with the sick child. We feel that this extra love made them well much more quickly than medicine could have. We have not had a doctor's bill for nineteen years. God is Love, and we believe that Love heals.

Our last three babies were born at home. It changed our views on many things. My husband discovered a new found joy in watching the baby sleep next to me so contented at my breast. He felt strongly that mother and babe need each other deeply and without disturbance the first few weeks after the birth. Baby slept a lot on my tummy during those early weeks.

These last three children, now ages nine, twelve, and fifteen, all slept in our bed from birth until they were about four years old. Then each voluntarily went to his siblings' rooms and beds.

Despite what some people may say about the results of this type of dependency on parents, our last three are very independent and very secure in many ways. We can see them all growing up to be loving, caring and feeling adults. We believe this is not something one can "teach" a child when he is grown. A child must live with loving adults in order to be able to live this way himself in the future. If people would only stop talking about love and instead love, there would be a big change in the world.

I remember being at a religious retreat where a young pregnant woman gave a speech on love. (She had left her other young children at home for three days.) I asked her if the new baby would be rooming-in with her at the hospital. To this she replied, "I want my rest. I will get enough of the bawling brat at home." If this mother can't show love to her own dependent little child, how can she speak on what she doesn't have at home? I believe that true love is that which overflows at home to spill out to others in the world.

By Mrs. S. who has five children, ages two through eleven years.

Many people have made comments on the child who always sleeps with his parents. They say that the parents will never get that child out of their bed, so why start something that can't be stopped? They also say you would have no personal life with your husband. We have found none of these theories to be true in our case.

Our fourth baby was the first child to be breastfed and to sleep with us. When she was about six months old she began waking at night. I'd take her to bed so she could nurse, and I usually fell asleep till the morning. As she grew older, she stayed longer till finally she was with us all night. After several years she slowly began sleeping with her older sisters. She rarely comes to us now.

The Family Bed

The fifth child has till now, age two and a half, slept with us since we brought her home from the hospital. It was not really planned that way. It all started on the first night after we came home from the hospital. Before we went to bed I nursed her and put her into her crib. She awakened at about two a.m. I took her into our bed then. It was great because we all got the sleep we needed. This became routine. She was a funny little one who would not go to sleep unless I lay down with her on the big bed. So I'd go to sleep too, at about nine p.m., and we'd have a good night's sleep.

We bought a side rail for the bed so that the baby could sleep on the outside of the bed without falling off, and I could sleep next to my husband. I would periodically ask my husband if he objected to having the baby in bed with us. I wanted to make sure that he knew that I did not prefer the child over him. But he always said, "No." One week our now two and a half year old child wanted to sleep with her sister and this she did. My husband commented then that he wasn't sure he was ready to have her leave us.

The joy of having the child in bed with us is that we truly enjoy it also. My husband and I find this our special quiet time together with our baby. We realize that nursing helps a mother feel close to her baby. We feel that this closeness and an understanding of the child can further develop when the child sleeps with his mother. My husband feels that having the child sleep in the parental bed has helped him, also, to develop a certain closeness and understanding between himself and the child. These feelings have in turn transferred to the older children who did not sleep with us.

We have found that if the child is not pushed out of the family bed prematurely, he will voluntarily begin to leave it when he is ready. We feel he is ready when he can be given a gentle encouragement to sleep in his own bed or with his brother or sister, and he accepts the change.

My husband and I feel we now have a closer relationship with our children. We only wish that our older children had slept with us. Nevertheless, we feel very fortunate to have had the chance to discover how very special this sleeping arrangement is.

By Mrs. A. who has six children, ages two through thirteen years.

It is morning, and I should feel so happy. Our firstborn arrived last night—a good delivery, and he is fine, thank God. But I have a big lump in my throat. If I did have a baby, why isn't he here beside me? Maybe I'll just call the nursery and see if he's okay. "Of course he's fine," a cool, surprised voice said. Now I just feel foolish for worrying, but the tears are welling in my eyes—and I want to hold him and be sure.

This evening our second child was born, easily and beautifully. I feel so happy but so restless. Maybe I'll walk down to the nursery window and look at her. "What! Are you down here again for the third time? You need your rest—go back to bed and sleep. You can hold her in the morning!" But I'm trying, and sleep won't come. My arms are too empty, and she seems so far away.

We've just had our third child—a big, healthy girl. This time I'm getting used to the routine around here. I am tired. So I'll forget about my baby and get some rest, if I can. (But I wonder why they always take my babies away as though I delivered them just to get rid of them.)

Our fourth baby is here, born a little after midnight on Christmas day. She was the only one I knew in the whole delivery room, and I called out, "I love you"—then felt so foolish 'midst all these strangers who smiled. At least this time they've promised me I can nurse the first day and not wait three days like I had to with the others. Guess I'll just have to reconcile myself to another restless night—why can't I relax like you're supposed to? My heart is overflowing with gratitude for this beautiful Christmas gift, but there's a funny ache there too— one doesn't loan her precious gifts out right away.

Oh joy of joys—our fifth child has at last arrived, and his Daddy and I shared this glorious time together. Now they want to take our baby away—hospital routine, you know—but we've begged to hold him a while longer. The nurse walked away shaking her head as though we were such stubborn people. Isn't he beautiful—isn't he perfect—isn't our love grand? Oh yes! Imagine, a whole hour we held him. Time stood still!

Sixth child of ours, you are a treasure, nursing at my breast, cradled in my arms, lying on me, sleeping by my side. Let's etch this calm and peace forever into memory. They say you can't tell where I stop and you begin. I feel so close to God and all of creation! It's the Seventh Day, and I'm resting, and All is Good.

All of our birth experiences were happy ones, in that I was awake and aware, heard our babies' first cries, and saw them right after they were born. It's interesting to me, though, that my ways of baby care at home reflected the way in which I was or was not allowed close contact with our babies in the hospital—almost as if I were programmed in a certain direction. (Naturally there were other factors too, such as the changing cultural climate, the reading that I did, and the support and examples of friends.)

With our first one I was more a "thing"-oriented mother. Even breastfeeding was a "business"—ideally a regulated number of hours apart, a set amount of minutes by the clock at each feeding. It was a ritual of hand and nipple washing, much as I had been taught in the hospital. Lots of baby equipment seemed essential, and when our firstborn was put to sleep in his very large crib and did not seem happy about it, I interpreted his cries as rejection of what we had to offer. (And deep down inside I felt very inadequate and frustrated as a mother.) But we persevered in trying to keep him sleeping often and long in his crib. I would stand beside him and hold a pacifier in his mouth trying to get him to fall asleep and stay asleep. Interestingly, at five months he spit the pacifier out and adopted his thumb, which lasted many years.

In a sense, although I did not let our babies cry without some attention, I literally forced our first ones to "mother" themselves through the long night. I remember well how very tired I was the first few weeks after our first child's birth. I would quickly climb into my own bed whenever I thought I had him sleeping. If he soon awakened, I felt resentful at my missed rest. Having him sleep through the night without a feeding seemed especially important. I pushed for this at seven weeks by offering him his pacifier instead of a feeding when he awakened toward morning. All these devices seem ridiculous to me now. How much easier it would have been for me and happier for both of us to have rested and slept together. But at the time this really seemed like a terrible "no-no." (Although I realize now this was just a cultural hang-up, and not a natural one.)

24

La Leche League had entered my life before our fourth child was born. I was allowed to nurse my baby soon after birth. I did relax a lot more at home and breastfed oftener and longer and always rocked and nursed her to sleep. I often fell asleep myself in the rocking chair. She was also the first baby that I carried around in a baby carrier. I began to experience a deep sense of rightness about being this close to my baby. However, it wasn't until our fifth child that I discovered the utter relaxation of nursing lying down and the closeness and peace this creates between mother and baby. I took many naps with him and when he would wake up for a while after going to sleep at night, it just seemed the best and most natural thing in the world to bring him to our bed until morning. By the sixth child I knew and deeply felt that baby belonged with me day and night. My husband and I just assumed she would spend her waking time close to me and her sleeping time by our side. I look on this interlude as one of the rewards of having children and am very grateful for having experienced it before it was too late. Not only did it seem to be the right thing to do, it was also very pleasurable and satisfying to have her close to us at night. I feel she knows her Daddy better too from sleeping close to him (in a way like osmosis).

Should we have more children we would continue the pattern that we followed with the last one. Naturally there are regrets for many of the ways we cared for our first ones and the lonely feelings they must have experienced. I recall with sorrow a lonely little three year old trying to come in with us at night and being hustled immediately back to *his* bed. . .and an unhappy four year old being scolded harshly to stay in bed and go to sleep without any sensitivity on my part as to what was bothering her. But these times are past, and today is what counts most in loving our children. Because of the good experiences with the last babies I now feel more sensitive to the needs of all of our children.

And it is easier to "make up" for a closeness which they missed as babies. Especially at bedtime such things as backrubs, hugs, kisses, or lying down in their beds and visiting seem very beneficial. I no longer think in terms of "my" bed. If the nine year old has a bad dream and wants to lie by us for a while or sleep there that night, it seems right to let her do so. If the two year old is still sleeping with us for most of the night, it seems quite okay to have her there also. All in good time she will wean herself from us and prefer to be with the older ones.

Author's experience. Two children, ages four and six years.

Gently I put our newborn baby down in the beautiful wicker basket. "There," I said, "this is your very own little bed, made by your grandmother." I gave the little silver birthbell a shake. It sounded sweet to my ears. The birthbell had first rung for my mother's birth, sixty years ago, then for mine, and now for the first grandchild.

For a few nights the baby slept right next to my side of the bed. It was a strange and wondrous feeling that overwhelmed me so strongly with this first child. It was all so new, and yet I had the feeling that it really was not new at all. I had never nursed a baby and yet I felt as if I recognized the feelings. I had never put my hand on a baby's head, and yet it felt so familiar. I had never had a baby sleep so close to me, and yet I felt it was very much a "right" happening.

After a few nights, my husband and I decided to move baby Yvonne out of the bedroom at night. She made so many little noises, and it kept both of us awake. We slept better. Yet, I felt that something was not right. I did not recognize this feeling. It puzzled me. It frustrated me. I felt strangely separated. But it was to take over two years before I again recaptured that recognition of quite a "right" feeling which I had had when she slept next to me.

After about a week, the problem of getting Yvonne to sleep began. I would nurse her until I thought she was sound asleep, then ever so carefully put her into her bassinet. Soon she would begin to cry. We jiggled the bed, tried a pacifier, sang songs, even rolled the little bed back and forth. "Is something wrong with her?" Night after night, week after week, it always took a long time before she finally fell asleep.

But, time does pass, and when she outgrew the bassinet, we moved her into a crib.

Unfortunately, due to the layout of our apartment, her bed-

26

room was separated from our bedroom by two hallways, and a large kitchen. We had to use an intercom at night to be sure to hear her when she awakened for her night nursing. We greatly disliked the idea that our connection with her was by way of a wire. How far removed we were. I frequently felt, after she had gone to sleep, that we had no child until the following morning.

The struggle of getting her to sleep continued. We tried the "crying it out" method. But after two weeks that still did not work. "This cannot be right. There must be another way. But what?" I was near tears. I was all tied up inside. "Yes, we have a child who has much difficulty in falling asleep," we told other mothers, hoping for a miracle solution.

The thought even crossed my mind that if I could crawl into the crib with her and nurse or sing her to sleep, she would not awaken when I moved away from her. I was so close to the solution. Yet, through cultural conditioning, it did not occur to me to take down the crib, and either take Yvonne into our bed, or put her on a mattress on the floor.

When she was almost two years old, we moved into our own home. I was seven months pregnant with our second child. We allowed our little girl to sleep with us for the first four nights in the new house. This will get her accustomed to the new surroundings, we thought. Although we felt somewhat strange those four nights, a little of the "right" feeling came back. But, even though it seemed so right, custom dictated that a child sleep in his own room, in his own bed. On the fourth day we spent much time upstairs in her room so that she could get used to her room, we thought.

Nighttime arrived. We went upstairs and rocked in the rocking chair for a while. Then I told her, "Now you *have* to go to sleep in your own room." I put up the crib gate so she could not climb out, and went downstairs.

She screamed. She cried, "Mama, Mama." She pleaded, "Mama come, Mama come." I came, but only to tell her that she had to go to sleep.

I went downstairs in the basement to iron some clothes. I kept looking at my watch. "She needs me. She needs me," said part of me. I ironed hard and fast. "Oh, that girl," said another part of me. "Why doesn't she go to sleep?"

27

I felt guilty, frustrated, helpless, overwhelmed, and I blamed her.

At last, silence. Cautiously I went upstairs, and as I stood by the crib, I saw a little, lonely child lying on her stomach, still quietly sobbing in her sleep. It took about a week before the nightly agony had dwindled down to a quarter of an hour.

Since the baby was going to be born soon, my husband and I discussed what we might do in order that Yvonne could sleep through the night. We had been told that most of the time night waking in toddlers was nothing but a habit. Although we did not really believe it, we thought we would try to "break that habit." But it did not work, and after three nights we decided it just was not worth the unhappiness. We would manage somehow after the baby was born.

Michelle was the third occupant of the beautiful bassinet. (The second baby was my brother's infant son.) We have a photo of Michelle sleeping in the little bed. "You only slept here for short naps during the day," reads the caption. "At night you slept with Mama." Michelle, too, would not sleep in the bassinet for very long without waking. By this time, however, we had learned a lot. We had talked to other people who had taken their children into bed with them. Michelle became a regular bed partner from birth on. We never have, so far, had any bedtime problems with her. I lie down with her till she is asleep and then quietly move away. What a difference from our first experience.

When Michelle was three months old, Yvonne, almost two and a half, wanted to go to sleep in our bed. We tried to persuade her otherwise, but she insisted. We decided then that if it meant so much to her, why not? Really, why not? She went to sleep in our bed. Later in the evening we took her upstairs into her own bed. After fourteen days she began to awaken as we moved upstairs. She would cry and cry till she finally fell asleep in her crib. One night she screamed uncontrollably. I applied wet cloths to her face. I rocked her. I sang to her. The tension mounted and finally her screaming overwhelmed me, and I exploded with one horrible scream, "Stop it!" A moment of shock. A moment of silence. Then she lay her tear-drenched face against my shoulder and whimpered. And I felt so guilty, so exhausted, and so helpless. Was this endless struggling ever going to stop?

On that night Yvonne rejoined our family bed. The going-to-sleep problems gradually diminished. We enlarged our bed, and felt greatly encouraged that what we were doing was right.

One day I told Yvonne that whenever she cried again, we would offer to hold her till she felt better. A small miracle then happened. A wall between us seemed to fall away. That night she slept very close to me, and has done so ever since.

We feel very close now. We feel so fortunate to be able to experience this for a few years. I have been asked numerous times if it is not bothersome to have our children sleep with us. To this I reply that it is no more bothersome than their presence in our family.

As I sit here writing, our German Shepherd dog stretches out and sighs. Papa is reading, and our two children are sound asleep in the family bed. Later we will join them. How can I express this feeling of utter fulfillment? I am a mother! I will protect and touch you children during the stillness and darkness of the night. I will spread my love and cover you with it. What loveliness can surpass this?

I look at the silver birthbell. Six years have passed. When it rings again, it will be for a new generation. I hope it will ring of the happiness that took me two years to learn, but which I will now treasure forever.

WHY SOME PARENTS HESITATE

. . .it appears to be the fashion these days
to disrupt all inherited patterns and to defy
in a million small ways what nature seems
bent on preserving. *
*　　　　　—Kenneth L. Woodward*

We enjoy being together when we are eating. We enjoy sitting together on the couch, reading. We enjoy going to church together. We enjoy sitting huddled together around a campfire, singing, talking, reminiscing, or just looking at the dancing flames, listening to the quiet sounds of the night. We enjoy walking together, side by side, or going for a ride, or silently sharing the beauty of a seascape.

We receive encouragement to do all of these things together. The family that plays together, prays together, will stay together. Yet when it comes to sleeping together we bounce headstrong into opposition.

NATURE vs. CUSTOM

Separate sleeping rooms constitutes a relatively new phenomenon which is found mostly in the Western world. But as much as this custom enjoys a rather large following, it is not without some discord. Authorities have recently overwhelmingly cautioned against taking children into the parental bed. Yet, parents are doing it.

31

There is a natural drive or instinct which outweighs this advice. This is significant. It indicates that the advice needs considerable re-evaluation. Indeed the Grand Mere of anthropology, Margaret Mead, in personal correspondence with the author stated: "The fact that co-family sleeping occurs regularly in many human groups as it does among ours even though the social code is opposed to this practice, is highly significant, and points to a stubborn human characteristic which is worth following up."

The resulting conflict of nature vs. social custom is an aspect of childrearing which has unfortunately caused much undue frustration and unhappiness. On the one hand parents receive insufficient encouragement, or none at all, for total parenting, e.g. answering every emotional need of the child. Breastfeeding and sleeping with his mother are a child's basic emotional needs. Also, many marital beds are simply too small to accommodate comfortably more than two people. The rule holds that children are just not taken into the parental bed.

On the other hand, there is an inner drive in parents which forces them to overlook all this and take in the children anyway. The parents are thus pulled between two strong forces. And in the effort to work out a practicable solution, they are sometimes disappointed, frustrated or sad about the outcome. It would be so much simpler if customs favored total mothering and co-family sleeping. Not to do it may lead to unhappy family members. To do it may require head-scratching or uncomfortable nights, and the result in some families is an unhappy situation. Nature dictates one way. Society says another. And the consequence can be frustration, with in many cases, the happiness of the family at stake.

"This has probably been the most difficult problem we have faced with our child," writes a mother. The child wanted to sleep with the parents. The parents wanted to welcome her, but were afraid that it would be harmful.

Dr. Lee Salk admits that even though psychoanalysts have been very firm in their recommendation that parents should NEVER allow children into their beds, his experience tells him that very few parents are able to abide by this rule in an absolute fashion.[1]

NEGATIVE ADVICE

If we turn to literature for parental guidance we get rather unsympathetic advice, which, nota bene, changes over the years to go along with whatever the current times demand and will tolerate.

In a popular pamphlet of 1967, *Infant Care*, distributed freely to new mothers we read:

> It is a good idea to start the baby out with sleeping arrangements you can keep throughout childhood. This means that you'll expect him to sleep alone, in his own bed. Babies are noisy roommates. You lie awake, waiting for the next gurgle or snort, wondering if he's going to cry or not. It's hard to get the sleep you deserve. Baby finds it pleasant to have you near, and may decide to move in. (*Even the authors of this publication realize that it makes baby happy. —Author's comment.*) He'll do his best to make it a regular thing. And a permanent bedfellow, especially one who is apt to wet the bed, becomes a pest. You're sure to resent it eventually, and the baby will be even more troubled by your refusal to let him in with you.[2]

And thus you are welcomed, precious infant!

It is not my goal to "put down" and criticize popular books on childrearing. However, in order to try to understand why parents hesitate in taking their children into bed with them, I feel I must make some reference to passages of those books which many parents use as a guide.

The passages give parent-oriented advice, and destroy any incentive on the parents' part to follow their God-given instinct. And who will not find it difficult to counter a popular precept, even though it may go against an inner response? A response, it must be noted, which came about by an actual bodily, physical change caused by the mere fact that one has become a biological parent.

Some parents hesitate in taking an unhappy baby or child into bed with them because early examples and childrearing books have greatly interfered with their natural reaction to the cry.

The routine of schedules and the piteous crying of the infant that goes along with it are all too often considered to be normal and inevitable. One of the books which attempts to give mothers a picture of what a typical, healthy baby is like describes a usual hospital nursery scene: "He cried hard in the nursery, filling his stomach with gas."[3] Just as it was time to be wheeled in to his mother for a feeding he had fallen asleep, exhausted.

After the mother comes home, she reportedly realizes that his fussing at home is a carryover from not having fit into the routine of the hospital's schedules, and that he had cried and been miserable in the hospital also.

The author leaves the description at that. He seems to ignore the fact that a crying baby needs relief. Instead, he suggests that the crying is nothing about which to worry.

It is not surprising, then, that mothers wonder if they are perhaps wrong in feeling anxious and upset at hearing their child in distress.

Further on in the book the author soothes any concern by stating that the baby will sort out and obliterate the unpleasant moments anyway, so his crying doesn't matter.[4] This statement is continually being disproven. The mind perceives, records, and remembers everything from birth on, if in fact not from life *in utero.*

Granted, the healthy mind tends to focus on remembering the more pleasant aspects of life. However, the unpleasant happenings are recorded, nonetheless, and are there to stay.[5]

Why do parents hesitate? If they have not read any of the numerous books on childrearing, then certainly they have leafed through a copy of the Dr. Spock's *Baby and Child Care.*

Among many middle class families in the United States, a well-used copy of this book has replaced the *Holy Bible* by the bedside. His book has been translated into over twenty-nine languages, and by 1968 over twenty-one million copies had been sold in the United States alone.[6]

"Better not let the child in your bed," he recommends. Then he gives as reason that when such a child has been picked up and treated to company for a number of nights, he learns to rouse himself from half awake to wide awake to have more of the fun.[7]

Eating when one is hungry is fun too, but it certainly is also a very basic necessity. Wanting and needing to be near someone (and a baby's wants and needs are one and the same thing), is an equally important drive that needs to be fulfilled.

"Sometimes," Dr. Spock says elsewhere in his book, "the parents take a frightened child into bed with them so that they can all get some sleep." But this, he feels, usually turns out to be a mistake because the child may "cling to the security of his parents' bed,"

34

even if his immediate anxiety decreases.8 "So *always*," he concludes, "bring him promptly and firmly back to his own bed."

Who will speak for the child?

"Why start something you cannot continue forever?" another doctor wrote to me. Forever? Yes, that would be a long time. But, does it last "forever"?

Let us now listen to what a parent has experienced. "It is interesting to observe that after traumatic or insecure times in our family, such as after a trip or during illness, we have a great deal of bed-hopping. After a few weeks, however, all settles down again and the children come to us about once a week."

Parents should be given the glory and the pride that *they* are whom the child seeks in time of need; that to the child they are more important than all the toys and teddy bears and dolls and blankets; that *only they* can give *true security* to him.

It is sad that it is considered to be manipulating when the child tries to convince his parents that he would rather be with them than with his toys.

I feel that we could label a child's actions manipulative when he seeks a purely material gain. For instance, the child who embarrasses his mother by screaming in the supermarket because he wants to have some candy. However, when a child's behavior is such that it requires purely human attention, he has a need to seek fulfillment of an emotional or physical want.

After the young one has been subjected to automatic infant swingers, factory-produced glass bottles and rubber pacifiers, play-pens, baby-sitters, and day care centers—when everything has been done to find substitutes for the parents, can they, his parents, not at least and at last be given the credit for being the ultimate form of security for their offspring and fulfill that part of their parenthood?

One sad story which was told to me referred to a couple who had followed the advice of never allowing their child into their bed. But since the child was so persistent in getting out of his own bed, they locked their bedroom door one night.

The following morning they found him curled up and asleep against the outside of their bedroom door. Their child went as close to his parents as he could.

But today's ideal is a meticulous, pretty, attractive room for each child. A room which has children's pictures on the wall, cuddly teddy bears that play little tunes, soft dolls that wind up and say "Hold me tight," numerous toys and a little night light to keep the world from disappearing at night.

Pretty? Certainly! But, Mommy, it is so lonely.

Even while admitting that his advice is not definitely harmless from a psychological point of view, Dr. Spock nevertheless goes ahead with a suggestion for handling the insistent toddler.

When a climbing-out-of-bed problem in a two year old has gotten completely out of hand, he suggests that the parent rig a string netting over the top of the crib. He urges that it should never be spoken of as a punishment or a threat. The mother can suggest it cheerfully as a top on the bed to make a cozy house for the child to stay in and sleep in. She can ask the child's help in tying it on.9 No word is spoken, however, about what happens after the cheerfulness wears off and the real reason for his climbing out of bed arises again.

And all this misery simply because of that taboo: "Don't take your children into bed with you," misery because we are urged to go against a basic human need. We are bombarded by suggestions that evil and terrible things are going to happen when we take the children in with us. The subject of sex is exposed. Consequences are mentioned such as overdependence, homosexuality, neurosis. And whenever possible, samples are given of a Dr. so-and-so who knows of several neurotics, (or homosexuals, or persons who are overly dependent) who "aha, slept with their parents or siblings till they were in their teens."

But when these same unbalanced persons jump in and out of bed ten times to make sure the doors are locked, that no tigers are hidden in the closet, or are never quite sure if they turned off the stove, then they may be labeled as ones who have a certain set of bedtime rituals.

Indeed, some people with psychological problems may have slept with members of their families. And certainly an unfavorable family situation may have led to a neurosis. However, is it fair to stress continually co-family sleeping and its association with neurosis? Recently an article on disturbed children appeared in a child psychiatry journal. It stated that over eleven percent of the children in

36

a particular institute were recorded as sleeping with their parents. The article did not stress, however, that a significant majority did *not* sleep with their parents. At least their sleeping patterns were not coded. Should the connection between co-family sleeping and emotional problems be indeed so strong, then sleeping together within the family would, according to this study, hold a most favorable position.

Other negative advice urges parents to place their own comfort and importance first. Yet parents are willing to discard this advice once they have tried co-family sleeping, and have seen the results. And what is more, once they have tried it, they don't *want* to change and their children are happier too.

One mother wrote that before her first child was born she read all the "right" books, in order to prepare herself for rearing her children. "I had simply memorized 'a crib is for sleeping, and a playpen is for playing.' We thought that separate beds was the way to do it—society's demand that they would have to learn sometime! We did not last very long though," this mother continued, "when we realized that we were developing clinging preschoolers during the day, especially during the morning rush.

DRUGS FOR SLEEP

Drugs are used to suppress lactation. Drugs are used to suppress fatigue. Drugs are used to suppress emotions. And drugs are used to cause sleepiness, even in children.

Today, say Luce and Segal, there are over thirty million Americans who cope with anxiety, insomnia, tension, and emotional distress by taking drugs—often without close contact with their doctors. There seems to be a strong and most dangerous sleep myth that insomnia can be cured by simply swallowing a pill.[10] This popular uneducated conception has persuaded many, incorrectly, that sleep is purchasable at any price. Many actually believe that a pill will cure rather than mask the underlying cause for sleeplessness. Some parents will insist on sedatives for their child when he does not fall asleep at pre-determined schedules.[11]

That the advice for drugs to induce sleep in an apparently normal child who is having difficulty in falling asleep should actually be given by a twentieth century doctor leaves me greatly discouraged. It is most frightening that these dangerous drugs are given to children where love, compassion, and companionship would have given much better results (without the risks of drugs). Nevertheless though, one doctor advises in his book on child care that if the firm approach mixed with a dose of compassion is not successful, the parent may ask the doctor for medication. There is nothing wrong with doing this, he feels.[12] And thus we begin early teaching that life's problems can be solved with a pill. How far-removed have we become from clean, fresh, healthy, happy living?

Everything possible is suggested to the parents to prevent the child from entering the parental bed and to keep him in his own; even to the point of drugging him into a state of unconsciousness which is supposed to be a good night's sleep.

And yet, a natural force naggingly persists in opposing even this method. The child may be asleep now. But what will tomorrow bring?

PARENTS HESITATE

Following is a list of reasons given by parents as to why they at one time or another hesitated in taking their child or children in to bed with them.

- I need my sleep.
- We all slept better when the children slept in their own beds.
- I was more confortable sleeping alone.
- Husband was against it.
- Bed is too small.
- Room is too small for a larger bed.
- Because custom indicated it should be this way and gave no alternative.
- Complete ignorance.
- Baby too active physically.
- Books.
- Relatives said, "You'll be sorry!"
- Pediatrician's advice that baby should not come between parents, in bed or otherwise.
- Mother too active in sleep, awakened children and husband.
- Baby made too many noises.
- Afraid that we would roll on baby.
- Interfered with sex.

- Awareness of baby made me sleep less soundly.
- Afraid to make him too dependent.
- Afraid that we would not be able to break the habit.
- Baby's wetting the bed and vomiting bothered us.
- We thought it better to show consistency from birth on.
- My doctor told me my baby might get an earache if I lie down and nurse him.

In the *Childbirth Education Association News Letter* of Greater Minneapolis-St.Paul, Minnesota, August 1973, an article by Dr. William G. Crook reports on the increase of ear infections in babies over the past twenty years. "Formula allergy was first blamed," he states. "But recent research strongly suggests that the blame be put on the fact that babies get fluid in their ears because many of them take their bottle lying down."[13]

The article further comments on the "frequently made observation that ear trouble is uncommon in breastfed babies." Whether he is being nursed in a chair or in bed, the breastfeeding baby is frequently lying in a horizontal position, and on his side. Breastfeeding mothers need therefore not fear that their baby will necessarily get an ear infection when being nursed in bed.

Another negative reason which concerned parents was the supposed connection between caries in a child's teeth and night nursing. The following question is by a mother of a nursing two year old.

HELP! I have a two year old who wakes several times during the night. This has not bothered me, nor has sleeping with us bothered us. But now he has eight cavities. I've been told by a number of dentists that this is due largely to night nursing. Those who have not actually suggested I stop nursing, have told me I must face the problem of future cavities in great number. Obviously dental work at this age will be traumatic, but so will stopping the night nursing. What do I do?

If indeed caries are due largely to night nursing, then the mouths of children throughout the world, and throughout history must have been in a frightfully deteriorated state. I believe that it is by now fairly well established that the state of our teeth is largely due to the kind of food we eat.

Many dentists now urge us to eat wholesome, unrefined foods, to stay away from sweets, eat fresh fruits and vegetables, and brush our teeth at least once a day. Therefore this toddler's problem was not the fact that he was breastfed or slept with his parents, but rather that his eating habits were conducive to the many caries. Ice cream, cookies, candy, sweetened teething biscuits and not enough fresh fruit and vegetables were most likely the real cause for the sad condition in the child's mouth. In the *La Leche League News*, 1972, p. 57, it is reported that "Breastfeeding can play an important role in solving some of the dental problems that plague American society." When carried out as nature intended, breastfeeding satisfies the child's sucking needs, both nutritionally and emotionally. La Leche League encourages total mothering which implies giving baby the breast for comfort as well as for food, both during the day and at night.

Children who are allowed to nurse freely and wean themselves when they are ready, may nurse until the age of three, four or five, and occasionally longer, just as some children may have a bottle or suck their thumb well past their first few years of life.

Whether during night nursing or day nursing, breastfed children frequently fall asleep at their mother's breast and remain there till the nipple easily slips out, or can be removed from the child's mouth.

Since co-family sleeping and late nursing are not the accepted practices in our Western culture, they are, unfortunately, quickly blamed for emotional or physical irregularities. Hopefully the day will come soon when this will no longer be the case.

SUDDEN INFANT DEATH SYNDROME

Then came there two women, that were harlots, unto the king, and stood before him. And the one woman said, O my Lord, I and this woman dwell in one house; and I was delivered of a child with her in the house. And it came to pass the third day after that I was delivered that this woman was delivered also; and we were together; there was no stranger with us in the house, save we two in the house. And this woman's child died in the night because she overlaid it. (1st Kings 3: 16 AV)

This Biblical passage points to the evidence that Sudden Infant Deaths have been with us since antiquity. That they were necessarily caused by "overlying" has been declared erroneous, however.

As some societies still practice today, mothers routinely used to sleep with their infants. When a mother awakened to find her child dead, she assumed she must have rolled over on him and caused his death.[14] But one author suggests that if indeed the death was caused by "overlying," the mother or wet nurse may well have been drugged or intoxicated.[15]

Because of this term "overlying," many mothers hesitate to sleep with their babies.

When we examine old medical books of the middle 1800's, however, we read that mothers were then urged to have their babies sleep with them. One of these books reads:

From the inability of the newborn infant to maintain its own heat, and the extreme care with which the lower animals protect their young against external cold, as well as from direct experience, there can scarcely be a doubt that, at least during the first four weeks, and during winter or early spring, the child will thrive better if allowed to sleep by its mother's side and cherished by her warmth than if placed in a separate bed.[16]

Another book of the past century advised that a child ought not to sleep alone until after he had been weaned, which frequently was not until the latter part of the child's first or second year.

As anyone knows, most people can learn to sleep through a repeated noise which has no specific meaning. The sound of cars, airplanes, trains, TV, usually doesn't bother a person's sleep if he is accustomed to it. But this same person may be readily awakened by an unusual squeaking of the floor. A mother may sleep through the blaring of a television set, but awaken instantly at the whimper of her infant. Perhaps a new mother possesses a sense which keeps her alert for her infant, even when she is "sound" asleep. A number of mothers whose babies sleep with them have told me they find themselves waking after several hours in the same position as they were when they went to sleep. Their mother instinct kept them on the alert even during sleep.

One mother wrote me that she and her husband kept dreaming that they were going to roll on their new baby. This comment is especially interesting since the child slept in a bassinet in another room. (The question arises as to whether parents who do sleep with their infant dream this also.)

According to the National Foundation for Sudden Infant Deaths, SIDS (Sudden Infant Death Syndrome) commonly known as "crib death," or "cot death," causes from 10,000 to 15,000 infant deaths annually in the United States.[17] One source, however, claims it to be as high as 25,000.

41

An apparently healthy baby, usually between the ages of three weeks and seven months, is put to bed without the slightest suspicion that things are out of the ordinary. Some time later he is found dead without any demonstrable disease. Often there is no evidence that a struggle has taken place, nor did anyone hear the baby struggling.

SIDS happens during naptime or during the night. Many theories as to the cause of SIDS have been put forth. None of these has been definitely proven and most have been discounted.

Theories that according to the National Foundation For Sudden Infant Deaths have been declared invalid include allergy to cow's milk, bacterial infection, radiation fall out, use of drugs, smoking, adding bleach to the diaper wash, air pollution, and fluoridation.

In their pamphlet, "Facts About SIDS," by the NFSID, sleeping with baby is not even mentioned as a possible cause for this tragedy.

This foundation further believes that there has not been an increase in the number of SIDS cases in recent years, but one hears more about them since there is currently more extensive publicity about them than has been true in the past.

Studies conducted by the foundation in many areas of the world consistently show figures of two to three SIDS deaths per 1,000 live births.

Many communities now do report the cause of death as Sudden Infant Death, or "crib death." Unfortunately, other areas still list them as suffocation or overlying which, the NFSID states, is a tragedy since it implies neglect or carelessness on the part of the family.

One such newspaper article urges all doctors routinely to caution parents against the "dangerous" practice of sleeping in the same bed with an infant. The article continues with the report of a study of 336 crib deaths in Shelba County, Tennessee. According to an investigator, twenty-four cases were *almost certainly* due to overlying and in another forty-nine cases it was a *very strong possibility*.[18] (Author's italics.)

When this article was brought to the attention of the La Leche League International Board of Directors, which suggests taking a nursing infant to bed, Mary White, a member of the executive board, answered that this study was out of date, and has been disproven by later study. (1971)

It is important to realize, says the National Foundation for Sudden Infant Deaths, that recent research indicates that Sudden Infant Deaths cannot be predicted. There is no known way to definitely prevent their occurrence.[19]

According to an article in a 1971 *La Leche League News*, however, breastfed babies are still rarely victims of the sudden-death syndrome.[20]

In all probability more breastfed babies than bottlefed babies sleep with their mothers. Still the incidence of SIDS among breastfed infants is lower than that among formula-fed children. Or, should we take the opposing view which says that breastfed babies have no lower incidence than bottlefed babies, "overlying" is still not mentioned by either side.

Consider also the probability that the greater majority of babies do not sleep with their mothers. It is significant to realize then that in spite of separate sleeping, it is nowhere mentioned that the rate of SIDS has dropped from a hundred years ago. At that time many babies slept with their mothers. Nor is the occurrence of Sudden Infant Death Syndrome higher in societies in which mother and babe routinely sleep together.

If we consider the infant himself, we see that nature has given him very strong means of survival. In some ways he is tremendously strong, his reflexes are superb, and he has a good voice.

When an infant lies on his stomach, he has a set of reflexes that make it almost impossible for him to smother in that position. When the free flow of air is threatened, he raises his head off the bed, and turns it from one side to the other. He begins to crawl with his legs, and can even lift himself up on his arms.[22]

When he lies on his side or his back, baby's arms are almost continuously flexed so that his little hands are close to his face, ready to push things away that threaten him. As any mother can testify, it is frequently difficult to bend a baby's arms to a straight position.

Investigators have further found, reports the NFSID, that even when infants are covered by bedding, the amount of oxygen is not reduced to the point of causing suffocation.[23]

When the child finds himself in an uncomfortable or alarming position he will certainly do everything possible to let the mother know of his distress by crying and kicking.

A mother of eight children wrote me the following: "One night I could not sleep and I decided to observe Baby. The infant was three weeks old, and sleeping between my husband and me. Baby was lying on her back, with her arms bent, fists close to her face. Father was sleeping too, but started to roll over onto the child. The infant immediately put out her arms and feet and began to whimper. In his sleep my husband reacted to the touch and sound and moved away from the child.

"I began to nurse her, and became further interested to see what would happen if I changed my position so that my breast fully covered her face, thereby inhibiting breathing. I changed my position and after what seemed minutes, the baby suddenly jerked her head away from the breast, gasped several times, and then was fine again. She resumed nursing."

Another mother told me of the incident when she moved too close to her tiny two-and-a-half-week-old son. She said that the baby protested so vigorously that no one could possibly have slept through it.

This mother and her husband, whose friends had lost a baby in crib death, found they slept much better knowing that their baby was with them.

If the fear of possibly harming the new infant creates such a mental anguish that neither the mother nor the father sleeps well, I feel that having baby in a cradle right next to mother would be a better solution. The mother can still feel that she is right there when her baby needs her, and she will not need to get out of bed to nurse her infant. Or if she is bottlefeeding, she can get the bottle, and then snuggle up in bed with her baby while she gives him his milk. After baby is put back in his little bed, the mother will be able to rub baby's back and gently rock the cradle while resting. She will still feel the closeness of her precious new one, which is indeed such a wonderful feeling. When the child is a few months old he can then be taken into the parental bed.

From the beginning of time till quite recently many infants slept with their mothers or mother substitutes. In many parts of the world this practice is still customary.

In the last seventy-five to one hundred years it has been the custom in the Western world to have baby sleep by himself. But as far as research indicates, there has been no drop in the cases of Sudden Unexplained Infant Deaths.

And so, as La Leche League's manual *The Womanly Art of Breastfeeding* reads: "When your baby wakes at night, you need only tuck him into bed with you, start nursing him, and the two of you can drop off to sleep together. It's quite safe—we've all done it, and baby loves the warm closeness which usually helps him drop off to sleep sooner than he might do otherwise."24

THE IMPORTANCE OF SLEEPING TOGETHER

You have touched me. I have grown.

A Kikiyu chief of East Africa once spoke these words: "At night when there was no sun to warm me, my mother's arms, her body took its place. . ."[1] What a truly beautiful feeling that both mother and child enjoy when they sleep together.

THE IMPORTANCE OF LOVE

Love is exchanged between people, not between people and things, because love is a two-way process in which a person not only gives but also needs to receive love.[2] In order for a person to be able to give and receive love freely as an adult, it has had to be necessary that he was able to give and receive love freely when he was a child.[3] Even the infant, says Montagu, is born not only wanting and needing to be loved, but also wanting and needing to love others. It is not adequate that he should have to transfer his giving to an inanimate article, because this thing does not give love in return.[4] And all evidence indicates, report Salk and Kramer, the newborn infant also has an impressive capacity to observe the world through his senses.[5] For too long it was erroneously believed that babies are rather dull and selfish creatures, only wanting and taking when they had the notion. This belief, says Montagu, has done a great deal of damage to human beings and to society.

Robbed of the presence of another person, a baby or young child who is strongly urged to fall asleep by himself and stay in his own bed at all times is forced, when the need arises, to "mother" himself at night. A thumb, bottle, blanket or teddy bear will take

47

the place of mother, of love. He may even suppress his need for mother or father at that time, and convince himself that he does not need her or him. Unfortunately, a suppressed need does not become a need erased, although it may lie dormant within the person for many, many years.

"It seems to be the law of nature," writes Ratner, "that human beings need a certain total amount of time and devotion from their mothers. If the mother does not give of herself to her child when the child is most dependent—a force which liberates the child to become independent by the security obtained—nature has a peculiar way of exacting compensation later in the child's history."[6]

Ours is now a society in which we give no second thought when we see a young child frantically clutching his blanket. We unquestioningly accept advice which urges separation of mother and child. Babies are left to cry or are given an article which serves as a mother substitute. Ours is now a society in which, according to Salk, more than half the hospital beds are filled with mental patients.[7] It is a society in which many adults are still struggling with unmet infantile needs of their own.[8] Ours is now a society in which many mothers and fathers have been left with frustration which results from an unfulfilled need, the need to be "the sun," to be the all-goodness giving source to the baby.

Mothers have told me that as much as they loved and cared for their children who were bottlefed and slept in their own cribs, there was frequently a feeling of, "Should I not do something more for them?" as they kissed their children good night. These mothers did not experience this feeling with their breastfed children, especially if they all slept together. They then felt total fulfillment.

True love should be free to be exchanged at any time, unconditionally, whether day or night. It is the freedom of exchange, the knowledge that there are no set times, that makes it beautiful and important.

The mother who at night takes her child into her arms and comforts him, and then peacefully falls asleep with her little one touching her body, knows and feels deep down that she is not only giving but that she is also receiving something that no words can describe. It is a feeling of knowing that she is being part of the universe, a link in the chain of life. She is forming a momentary oneness with her child which, as the need diminishes, will flower into a twosome again, much like the flowering at birth. A glow fills her body, and this glow radiates to her other children and to her husband. But this feeling of total fulfillment can only exist when there is no feeling of frustration or restraint.

In her keynote address during La Leche League's Fourth Convention, Marian Tompson, President, said, "I think we have much yet to learn about the special relationship between mother, father and child. I strongly suspect that loving parents protect the vulnerable infant in ways not yet understood from psychological and spiritual assaults as well as the more apparent and accepted ones. There is more there than the eye can see, or the mind understand at this point. It can be felt, especially by the breastfeeding mother in her oneness with her baby."

It has been observed, according to Montagu, that it does make some difference in the developing personality of the child whether or not he is breastfed and whether or not he is permitted to sleep in the same room or bed with his parents or siblings, and, "to enjoy all those experiences which result from such arrangements."[9]

The child is more demonstrative in showing affection, says Montagu, and seems better equipped to deal competently with social processes. Parents have verified that such a child also seems to have a higher degree of empathy for other members in the family. This can only graduate to a feeling of empathy for others outside the family unit, a compassion which would well help others in withstanding the impersonal pressures of our times.[10]

The ability to show this affection and understanding of others arises out of the satisfaction of self-esteem, which depends primarily upon a dependent relationship with the parents, and which necessitates during the first few years in the child's life the almost constant presence of other persons, preferably his mother, his father and his siblings.[11] La Leche League reports that studies show a direct relationship between the amount of mothering a baby gets and his physical and intellectual development.[12] Has it not been said that loving a baby is a lot like nurturing a plant? The more care it is given, the more fruit it bears.

The experience of sharing the same bed or bedroom results in a feeling of togetherness, of unity, of belonging.[13] It spreads love. A feeling of "I'm part of this family. I belong to you, to all of mankind" is perceived even while asleep.

Most fathers are gone during the day, the greater part of the child's waking hours. It will greatly help in the child's realization that Dad is an integral part of the family if he and Mom and Dad all sleep together. For one third of the day longer Dad is a real part of the child's life.

Sleeping together has a soothing effect on misunderstandings and harsh words spoken during the day. For an average of eight hours, in the stillness of the night, and the relaxing and disarming state of sleep, those who sleep together touch as if to say, "You are all right. I'm all right. We remain in touch with one another."[14] It is such a wonderful feeling to wake up in the middle of the night, and to kiss a loved one while he or she is asleep.

THE IMPORTANCE OF TOUCH

Montagu writes that physical contact "appears to act as a principle regulator of broodiness,"[15] which may be freely translated as meaning "mothering," or "parenting," (since men, too, may exhibit a certain amount of this behavior). Physical contact fulfills desires of that special feeling of parenthood, that wonderful feeling of closeness, and gives satisfaction to the protective instinct called mother-love, or parent-love.

Might this be one reason that once a woman has successfully nursed an infant, it is rare that she will want to bottlefeed again? And would it explain why parents, once they have had their children sleep with them, rarely reverse their decisions? Or that a new mother so instinctively treasures the contact with her newborn infant?

Unfortunately our society touches little. Even some breastfed babies, because of the mother's fear of criticism of "indecent" exposure, touch little of their mother's skin other than the nipple and areola.

Sleeping in the nude, or with the briefest nightgown, will compensate for some of this. The baby who sleeps with his mother thus clad, will lovingly carress and touch his mother, or manipulate or hold the other nipple while nursing. This seems to be a universal trait of the nursing child. I have observed this nipple holding in various photographs of nursing children in remote parts of the world.[16] And a number of my American friends have remarked on this action of their own babies.

If we accept the importance of continued cutaneous stimulation between child and parent,* then it becomes obvious that this ex-

---

*See *Touching: The Human Significance of the Skin* by Ashley Montagu.

change should not only take place between mother and her child, but also between father and his child. But in civilized countries such as ours, men are more fully clothed than women, and the actual chance of skin-to-skin contact is practically nullified. Add to this the fact that most fathers are gone during the greater portion of the child's waking hours, and it becomes clear that sleeping together would add considerably to the cutaneous interchange between father and child.

One mother wrote that her husband frequently slept with their baby on his chest.

Working mothers I have talked with have further suggested that sleeping with their baby and encouraging night nursings increased their mother-baby contact. Besides the obvious benefits to the baby, it also helped ease the mother's deep concern about her absence.

Karen Pryor, author of *Nursing Your Baby*, notes especially how beneficial it is for the child with neurological difficulties to sleep with his mother.

However, this tactile demonstration of affection between parents and their children, especially with children of the opposite sex, is frequently open to misunderstanding and ridicule.[17] It is frowned upon since touching in our culture is to a large extent associated with sex, and the great importance of the emotional transaction which takes place through the skin, by touching, has till quite recently been ignored. "This stress on the sexual element in all forms of intimate behavior," writes Morris in *Intimate Behavior*, "has resulted in a massive inhibition of our non-sexual body intimacies. When these intimacies apply to parents and offspring, then Beware, Oedipus!; to siblings, Beware, incest!; to close same-sex friends, Beware, homosexuality!; to close opposite-sex friends, Beware, adultery!; and to many casual friends, Beware, promiscuity!"

It is only since the 1940's, according to Montagu, that knowledge has been acquired and recorded of both the physical and emotional functions of the skin.[18] But as is frequent with scientific data, the initial research is far ahead of the general interest or acceptance.

In an article, "I'm Joe's Skin," published by *Reader's Digest* in 1972, many of the technical and physical aspects of the skin are mentioned, such as the complexity of the nervous system, the intricacy of the network of blood vessels.[19] But the emotional function of the skin, the subject to which Dr. Montagu dedicated a whole book, *Touching: The Human Significance of the Skin,* is not once brought to the attention of the reader. Dr. Montagu continually stresses the importance of touching the young child. He feels that it cannot be stressed too strongly that to be tender, loving and caring, to be considerate and understanding, to be able to freely give oneself to the needs of his offspring, one must have been shown consideration, understanding, and must have had all his needs fulfilled by a loving parent in his own earliest years, indeed from the moment of his birth.[20]

When joy from sadness, comfort from fright, are unconditionally experienced in the arms of his mother, or the proximity of other persons, the child learns to associate these feelings with people, and learns that he can turn to his fellow human beings in time of need.

Might it not be that persons turning to drugs are so discouraged and disappointed in other people, that they turn to a "thing" on which they can always rely? A thing that has no arbitrary restrictions placed on giving pleasure? Such as the "thing," the Teddy Bear, they could always turn to when they were children?

Perhaps we now see a repercussion with respect to this taboo of not touching and lovingly caring. Perhaps we now see an attempt to fulfill unfulfilled needs of that transition period of total dependence at birth to physiological independence at age three or four or older.

Today it is "the thing" for adults or older adolescents who cannot relate to others to try group therapy. Sensitivity or encounter groups have become popular from coast to coast. In some groups of sensitivity training, the persons are not allowed to talk with or even look at each other, but must communicate through touch. One is encouraged to embrace others, carress them, hold hands with them, bathe in the nude with them, and be massaged by them.

This is very, very difficult for most American adults. "One reason," says James Kenny, co-author of an article which appeared in *Marriage*, 1971, "is that our physical isolation from one another has been plotted since infancy. Single beds. Separate rooms. Stop fighting. Don't touch."[21]

Could it be that the popularity of communal sleeping in the communes is an attempt to seek a particular intimacy that was not fulfilled in infancy?

Or that the fun of teenage slumber parties is more than just staying up late, giggling, and pillow fights?

THE TRANSITION PHASE

The importance of co-family sleeping is further emphasized by its role in the transition period of an infant's total dependency on his mother, i.e. up to the moment of birth, and his physiological independence of her, usually by the age of three years or older. This is an aspect of childrearing which is, however, seldom considered in our Western culture; "indeed," writes Newton, "it may last less than one minute—until the cord is cut, before the delivery of the placenta."22

This transition phase is repeatedly present in those societies which seem to produce emotionally stable people. According to Newton, the fact that the components of this phase, namely close mother-baby contact (night sleeping), sensitivities to crying, child spacing and prolonged breastfeeding occur again and again in many of the primitive* and traditional cultures suggests that there may be a strong mechanism involved in this interrelation of patterning.23 It is important, therefore, to recognize and compare the effect which the presence or absence of the transition phase has upon the people involved.

In the primitive societies in question, unrestricted breastfeeding (therefore also night nursing) is nearly always present. Newton cites several sample cases in which breastfeeding takes precedence over any other activity in which the mother may be engaged, such as selling her vegetables in the market, although she may be extremely anxious to make the sale. Children are nursed freely, and frequently sleep with the nipple of the mother's breast in their mouths at night. The weaning process is slow and not usually before the age of two. Every attempt is nearly always made to soothe a crying child.24

People who emphasize the transition phase tend to feel strongly about the spacing of children. This spacing will insure the full energy and attention of the mother toward her child. Although frequent day and night nursing will in most cases lead to an absence

---

*Primitive people is used in its anthropological sense, meaning people who are without written language.

of ovulation for at least seven months,* and frequently up to eighteen, twenty-four or more months post partum, the concern of another pregnancy before the baby has reached a certain independent stage is so strong that many tribes keep a taboo upon intercourse until the child has reached this stage of development.[25]

The transition phase shows considerable variation among individual people and societies. But, as mentioned above, the fact that it occurs among most primitive societies which tend to produce stable individuals is an extremely important factor to consider.

Yet running counter to the fulfillment of the transition phase and the need for bodily contact is the modern trend toward minimum touching, early weaning, letting baby cry, and isolated sleeping, away from any other human being.[25]

These rather impersonal attitudes toward childrearing, by their emphasis on artificial substitutes for mother, have been the mode in the Western world since the middle 1800's.

According to Newton, the muting of the transition phase is one of the most striking differences between the primitive and traditional cultures, and our industrial culture.[27]

From the moment a healthy child is born, he is placed in a warmer, then a bassinet, then in a crib with a bottle, and encouraged to be by himself. This custom is to strong that many a mother worries tremendously when her baby seems to be in need of being held "so much," and when he does not seem to want to sleep by himself. The parent spends hours up at night because baby will not be put down in his bassinet without beginning to cry, and she is quite concerned when the infant at three months is still not sleeping through the night by himself. The "good" baby sleeps through the night. The "not-so-good" baby doesn't. It seems to be a status symbol, a sign of good mothering, when one's baby sleeps at night. "Does your infant sleep through the night yet?" is a question of great importance to some people, including doctors. "Is he happy?" is at times an afterthought, or is not asked at all.

Mothers who have their children sleep with them, however, are rarely concerned about nighttime waking. But aside from social pressures, it is no wonder that the mother who has to get out of her

*See "The Child Past Infancy."

nice warm bed should be so anxious for her child to sleep through the night.

"Why doesn't my child sleep through the night?" We hear the plaint of many a mother at many a tea party. Yet I believe there will be quite a few adults who can attest to waking up once or twice during the night, even if it is ever so slightly. When the child awakens then, perhaps as he turns over, he finds himself alone, and this is not well liked by little ones. He thus seeks his parents, just as during the day when he spends time alone with his toys, he will come running into the kitchen after a while for a hug or a kiss or just to say hello and lightly touch. Even little babies, like adults, awake slightly during their sleep. They will look around for a few seconds, and go back to sleep.

I overheard one mother tell another mother: "You know, my baby definitely sleeps longer when she sleeps next to me. Time and again it has happened that I would be resting with her when she took her nap. Several times during her sleep she would open her eyes, look right at me, turn around, and go back to sleep. When she has slept by herself, she would awaken and start crying when she did not see me. And that was usually the end of her nap." The other mother replied enthusiastically that her baby did exactly the same thing.

The outcome of a muted transition phase may, according to Montagu, result in individuals who lead lonely, isolated lives. They may even find it difficult to live close to others and touch freely.[28]

Perhaps there is a connection between the decreasing tactile relationship between mother and child, and the modern practice of husband and wife sleeping in separate beds.[29] May all this decrease in tactility in turn not be a contributing factor to the high divorce rate from which this country suffers?

BAD DREAMS

Young children may wake up screaming because of bad dreams. This may happen frequently as is the case with crying and temper tantrums; however we are repeatedly told how typical it is for them to have these bad dreams. Is this unpleasant experience really "normal"?

"Bad dreams and other night disturbances in sleep are frequently related to the child's fear of being deserted by his parents," says

Montagu.30 When a child sleeps with his parents, a sense of security is transmitted from parents to child. Likewise, children sleeping together transmit a certain sense of security.

Parents of large families, who have reared children both in the conventional way, and in allowing them in their bed, feel that sleeping together has definitely reduced the occurrence of bad dreams almost to the vanishing point. They have realized that co-family sleeping is a preventive measure, rather than a means of soothing the child, *after* he has already had his bad dream.

A mother wrote, "My son says he feels better if he is near me and can touch me when he has a bad dream which, since he has regularly been sleeping with us, is very infrequent."

Luce and Segal seem to feel that occurrence of nightmares is dream patterns. On the subject of nightmares in children they report that children may, during their deep delta sleep, scream and howl. They will fight off invisible monsters, shrieking for help and continuing to cry for their mother even when being held by the parent. The child is difficult to awaken from these terrifying dreams. He rarely remembers them.31

Luce and Segal seem to feel that occurence of nightmares is rather normal. It is interesting that parents' experiences seem to indicate that the child who sleeps by himself appears to have more nightmares than the child who sleeps in the secure presence of another person. Nightmares may be "normal" in the sense that they appear with relative frequency in our Western culture. Are they, however, normal in the sense of the process of human development?

Perhaps more research needs to be done on sleep patterns of the child who sleeps alone with a bottle (or any other mother substitute), the child who sleeps alone but is breastfed on demand, the child who sleeps with another member of the family in the same room, or bed, and the child who sleeps in bed with his parents until he reaches the emotional maturity to leave the master bed.

FEAR

The fear of being alone in a situation which is potentially or actually frightening or dangerous is real in most people. Darkness increases fear. Even in a situation which should not be frightening, such as sleeping in one's own bed, the imagination of both children and adults alike can play unpleasant tricks on the person. Thus sleeping alone, even though one may get used to it, may not feel quite as safe as sleeping with someone else. The sense of "He'll protect me. He'll help me. He'll hear it before I will," gives a sense of protection and safety and comfort. Many mothers have told me of the sense of fear they experience when their husbands are out of town for a few nights.

The feeling of fear of being alone may cause insomnia, or difficulty in falling asleep and remaining asleep. Likewise the feeling of loneliness may cause fear and overwhelm a person so that he cannot fall asleep. Fear, loneliness, and difficulty in falling asleep seem to be interrelated.

Sleeping together can therefore greatly reduce or alleviate fear. Much reference is made in Bowlby's book *Separation* to the reassuring effect the presence of a companion has on a person when he is in the dark or in a dangerous situation. This occurs both in animals and in human beings.[32] It is especially present in young children. The immediate reaction of a person who experiences fear is to seek out another person and to stay with that person for a considerable length of time after the fear has passed.[33] Thus co-family sleeping will not only reduce fear, but will have a continual calming effect after danger, whether real or imaginary, has past.

THE MIND PERCEIVES WHILE ASLEEP

Sleep was once considered to be a state of dullness, of deadness which was, however, something unavoidable and necessary, but nonetheless rather wasted as far as any usefulness with respect to learning and experiencing was concerned. Indeed, many a poet has likened sleep to death by referring to it as "eternal sleep."

> *Downy sleep*
> *Death's counterfeit*
> *—Shakespeare*

Until recently, state Luce and Segal, not much attention was given to sleeping behavior by anthropologists while they studied the living habits of other people. At night everyone just simply went to sleep, and studies were resumed the following day.

Child therapists usually do not bother to obtain information concerning the patient's sleeping history, even though valuable information could be revealed by doing so.[34]

That the mind is certainly not inactive and does perceive while asleep is proved by the fact that a person can learn while asleep. The science of "Hypnopaedia," which is learning while asleep, is a part of the repertoire of scientific literature. When during the 1950's sleep researchers began to demonstrate that human sleep follows a rhythmic pattern varying from light to very deep sleep, they banished forever the common notion that one part of the night is just like any other.[35]

One does not simply "go to sleep and wake up" in the morning. Even deep sleep is not like a coma. And children asleep are not dead to the world. Laboratory studies have shown that it is possible to listen during sleep, and to discriminate among sounds. Children and babies may not consciously remember what goes on during their sleep, but, say Luce and Segal, we no longer assume that they were untouched by the fights, conversations, and commotions that went on during their sleep. So too, a warm, loving atmosphere has an important effect on them.

Much yet needs to be learned about sleep, for it is an integral part of life's rhythm and relevant to every aspect of it. But children do not wait for scientific discoveries. Their needs are now. Ten years from now will be too late. And what simpler task could be asked than to give our time, love, and security to our children while we are asleep!

A NEED TO BE UNDERSTOOD

"It should be emphasized," said Edwina Froehlich, one of La Leche League's founding mothers, "that the willingness to accept the idiosyncrasies of parenthood, which are very different from the state of childlessness, are the first real signs that the person is ready to accept the obligations of parenthood."[36]

Many parents have rather unbending ideas about what a small child should be like, what he should have, and when he should have it. "Most parents will not admit," says Chisolm, "that these are really only matters of convenience for themselves or for the local custom, and that they have no real universal validity."[37]

Society has taken away the right of a baby to be dependent on his mother. Left to sleep by himself, states Salk, he often engages in self-mothering, in self-stimulation such as rocking back and forth, head-banging, thumb-sucking, fingering his ears, nose or hair.[38] He may even make a "nipple" out of a corner of a blanket and suck on it.

Among the non-literate people who generally give their children all the tactile stimulation they require, these forms of self-manipulation seldom occur.[39]

Yet some authors feel that it is a "right" of every human infant to have his own bed and bedroom;[40] they try to convince the parents that this is true. The needs of the person in question, the young child, are never considered. And to whom else can a statement like this be directed than to those few who can afford to give each child his own bedroom? As society becomes wealthier, human interaction becomes poorer.

We all have our need to be understood by others, intellectually, physically, as well as emotionally, and it is no less strong in the first few years of life. As adults we may tend to suppress certain needs at certain times. However, a child has not yet learned to do this. He usually will attempt to let his needs be known. Nor can a child wait very long for a need fulfillment. *A young child has an inborn safety valve which, if allowed to sound off naturally and freely, will announce when he can no longer remain in one particular state; that unless he gets relief, he will be carrying a burden which is heavier than is good for him. If he gets too cold, too hungry, too warm, too lonely, too frightened, the child will give indication that he needs a change, that he needs relief from the situation in which he finds himself. And the need for relief is now, not later.*

A child seeking the security of the parents' bed at night is indicating that he needs it as a change from a situation that upset him—cold, loneliness, fright, dreams. The child who sleeps with his parents needs only to move a little closer to his mother or father.

How do children learn to love? How do children learn to wait? Child psychologists' records of observations indicate that it is the baby who is immediately and unconditionally loved, who is immediately and unconditionally waited on, who learns to love and to wait. Indulgence in this respect at an early age results in patience as an adult. The person who is *not* frustrated in his early years, is capable of enduring frustration as an adult.[41]

We all feel overcrowded from time to time, and the idea of "peace and quiet" becomes very attractive. But human beings are social creatures who need one another, and for most of us a short time of solitude is sufficient.[42]

A young child has even less of a need for being alone; as a matter of fact, he usually does not *want* to be alone for very long. And when he does, it should be of his own choice, not ours. The young child cannot understand that giving and receiving of love should stop at nighttime, with lights out, and be resumed the following morning.

When a child of a very large middle class family saw that a neighborhood friend from a family of two had his own bedroom, he asked his mother if his friend was being punished by having to sleep all by himself.

It is lonesome to be alone, and most of us don't like it. It is wonderful to be close to others we love, and most of us thrive on it. The importance of co-family sleeping arrangements, be they parents and child, or child and child, lies in the fact that people thrive on being, literally, in touch with one another, even while asleep.

A united family in the true sense of the word is an asset to the strength of an individual and a nation.

NEED VS. HABIT

It is the law of human life, as certain as gravity;
to live fully, we must learn to use things and
love people. . .not love things and use people.
                                        —Maria Montessori

"It is not in the nature of nature," writes Salk, "to provide organisms with biological tendencies unless such tendencies have survival value."[1] It would therefore be wise to heed nature instead of trying to suppress or ignore it. Certain aspects of human life are not matters of opinions, but are determined biologically. The need of a child to sleep with members of his family is not a subject to be determined by our opinion, but should be determined by his emotional wants.

The wants of a well-adjusted human being are his needs. It is when his needs are not fulfilled that his wants become excessive in the attempt to fulfill suppressed needs.

We are born needing. We have need for air, food, sleep, and shelter. We have need for intellectual and physical stimulation. We have a need to be loved and touched.[2] If any of these needs goes fully or even partially unattended, the person hurts; and in the case of an emotional wound, the person may spend the rest of his life struggling to soothe the initial hurt.[3]

Gesell argues that a child passes through predictable stages of development at predictable times.[4] Thus what might seem to become a habit, may be simply a gratification of a need.

Hymes in his book *Child Under Six* describes a habit as an action

61

which can easily be broken. "If you run into any major difficulty at all," he writes, "BEWARE! You are probably not dealing with an old outworn habit. The chances are that you are tampering with a human need."5

If the body indicates a need for food, treating it like a habit and disregarding it will not make the hunger go away. Ignoring the sensation of wanting to lie down and sleep will not cure one forever from having to sleep eight hours a day.

But if one is in the habit of putting his keys in his right pocket, there need be only a worn out pocket to change the habit from putting the keys in right to the left pocket.

The child who seeks his parents' bed at night is expressing a basic need. And this need must take its own time and pace for satisfaction.

The child who is thus allowed to be with his parents will gradually mature to being satisfied with sleeping elsewhere, usually seeking the companionship of another member of the family. Should this child choose to sleep alone, it might do well to be aware that he has not transferred his seeking security from his parents or siblings to an inanimate object. If the child *wants* to sleep with his parents, it means he *needs* it. If he crawls into his parents' bed but then is content to be taken to a sibling's bed, it may mean that he was *in the habit* of going to his elders' bed.

For some strange reason we tend to think that to satisfy a child's need is to make it into an unbreakable habit, where in truth the exact opposite is true.6

When our children develop a "good" habit, one that suits us, we are afraid it is not going to last. But when our children develop a "bad" habit, one that does not suit us, we are afraid it is going to last forever. So many people are afraid that their children will not grow up. We are told to feed them solids with a spoon at three weeks of age, lest babies will never learn to eat solids, let alone with a spoon. We are told to toilet train them when they are one year old or they will never quit wearing diapers. We should begin to discipline them at one month, otherwise they will never listen to us. Children must always sleep in their own bed or they will always want to sleep with us. It is commonly believed that babies need to be weaned by the mother. And yet when weaning is left totally up to the child, it happens in a natural, healthy, relaxed way, usually between the age of one to four years. At the time the child no longer needs the direct physical contact with his mother, then he weans himself from the breast. Likewise, parents' experiences indicate that the healthy child will wean himself in time from the parental bed.

Children should be given the credit that, provided the home environment is healthy, they will mature. As each need is fulfilled at each stage, they will move on and become more mature. (We did. Let's hope.)

It will be found that one phase passes into another, and another, and another. Please trust that in a sound surrounding the child will graduate from each stage of development.

I remember carrying my first infant throughout the day. Then she began to crawl and I no longer needed to hold her so frequently. I remember nursing her fifteen times a day. Now she is weaned and eats and drinks what we eat and drink. I used to take her with me wherever I went. And if I could not take her I stayed home. (Except if she was asleep.) She was happiest with this arrangement. Then when she was about three years old, she took another step toward independence; she looked forward to the occasional baby-sitter to read her her bedtime story and put her to bed.

A child who has his needs fulfilled will become an independent, secure person. But indepencence cannot be forced upon someone.[7] It takes time and growing at the individual's own pace. The more secure he is in the knowledge that he can always come back to his parents, the more independent he will become. We will only create problems if we regard his needing us at night as a problem which should be "cured."

Our Western society is so complex. Our very houses are far too complex to let the child have the freedom of his domain. It is truly amazing how many restrictions we must place on him in his every day life. The stove is dangerous, the electric appliances are dangerous, etc. It is a real eye opener to count the number of times we say "No!" or remind a child that he is dealing with potential danger.

Should we therefore frustrate him even more by putting restrictions on emotional wants and needs?

The child's sleeping in the parental bed should not be regarded as a privilege, nor restricted for the fear of its becoming a habit. Rather it should be considered the necessary fulfillment of a basic human need.

BRIEF HISTORY OF CHILDHOOD
AND FAMILY SLEEPING

Learning is ever in the freshness of its youth,
even for the old.

—Aeshylus

"It is rather unimaginable," writes Luce, "that separate sleeping arrangements and bedtime problems with children are as old as mankind, and indeed they are not. They are products of our modern civilization."[1]

How is it then that we have chapter upon chapter, discussion upon discussion, frustration, counselling, questions, about a function which man has always performed, and which is so natural—sleeping? How have we come to the present situation?

Our subject, of course, is the child, and as we briefly scan the history of the child, we see that he has not always had the place in the family that he has now. He has risen from being considered simply an offspring who needs to outgrow his younger years before the level of a producing adult—now, quite a fuss is being made over him. He has moved from sleeping securely and snugly next to his family members, to sleeping isolated with a "snuggly" teddy bear.

MEDIEVAL TO 1700

Turning the pages of history back to medieval times, it may be observed by the viewer of the arts that until about the twelfth century children were rarely depicted as children. Rather they appeared as little adults, even to the extent of giving the naked

65

body of a child, in the very few cases when it was exposed, the musculature of an adult.[2]

It is rather doubtful that this was due to a lack of skill on the part of the artist, but more likely due to the fact that the child had no recognized place in the medieval world. This does not mean that he was not loved or well taken care of. He was just not accounted for. Early youth was considered a period of innocence which passed quickly and was just as quickly forgotten.[3]

The families living in one dwelling were usually large. It was common for the extended family, aunts, uncles, grandparents, plus servants, to live with the nuclear family. A child in this situation could easily be taken care of by others if his mother were not available. In a study on medical advice on childrearing of 1550 to 1900, Alice Ryerson shows that during the 1500's the child's dependency was given considerable encouragement. The swaddled baby was under constant attention and care. Mothers were greatly encouraged to nurse their babies. The child's cry was quickly responded to by either his being picked up and rocked, or breastfed. The child was allowed to remain in his mother's bed until he was weaned from the breast at the age of two or thereabout. But the weaning process was gradual. When he did finally move out of his parents' room, he was expected to move into a bed with his siblings or a servant. The gradual transition phase of this period closely resembles the earlier mentioned phase which most primitive societies hold or held.[4]

The great historical novel, *Kristin Lavrensdatter,* which is set in Norway around 1300 a.d. makes frequent mention of the co-family sleeping customs.

Around the thirteenth century, children entered the family portraits appearing more graceful and picturesque; a little closer to the modern concept of childhood.[5]

During the fifteenth century a change took place. The "child" was discovered. And from then on, although slowly at first, he became the puppet of child educators who made it their business to decide in every aspect what was best for him. These men were primarily moralists rather than humanists.

The youth's innocence was questioned. And the advice was given, although still far ahead of the times, that co-family sleeping and touching each other might lead to promiscuity. Girson, who, according to Aries, was the first representative of this "modern" thought, suggests, however, only that "it would be a good thing" that children start sleeping apart. He dared give no more than this suggestion because it was an overall custom that families slept together.6

Bedrooms as separate sleeping rooms as we know them were rare. For most people the bed was thought of as precisely what it is, a more or less comfortable place to sleep, usually built into the wall, or free standing with a curtain that could be drawn around it.7

During the reign of Louis XII in the fifteenth century, the French designed a bed for the king of such beauty that he held court and issued edicts from his *lit de justice*. The French nobility followed suit, and began to formally entertain their guests from high, elegant, elaborately canopied beds.8

But among the common people, the room in which the sleeping usually took place was either the large family kitchen, or another room in which other daily activities also took place. It is not an unusual scene in the paintings of 1500-1600 to see a family activity in the foreground, and, as part of the furniture, a four-poster, curtained-off bed in the background.

While still living in the Netherlands, I visited a number of quite old farmhouses. The beds in these dwellings were built into the wall, much like a closet. The door to these wallbeds was not only closed during the day, but at night as well. It is difficult to understand how anyone could sleep in the resulting stuffy air.

During the sixteenth century in England the so-called Trinity bed was developed. It consisted of a large bed upon which the immediate family slept. Two smaller beds, often referred to as trundle beds, rolled out from underneath the large bed. On this the servants and more distant relatives slept.9

In the seventeenth century, perhaps the largest of all beds was designed by John Fosbrooke for the royal family. It could sleep 102 persons! Obviously the "luxury" of separate beds and bedrooms of which we boast today was not at all considered to be a sign of wealth or prosperity during that time.

The attitude toward sex varies according to the accepted moral laws of the people. The gestures and jokes and sexual activities that took place during the 1600's without regard for the children's presence would shock the modern reader. This however was considered to be perfectly normal.10

The child under the age of adolescence was believed to be unaware of or indifferent to sex. This further explains why co-family sleeping created no problems. Whatever took place was morally accepted, and the children were reared accordingly.11 There is no written evidence," writes Ryerson, "that there were prohibitions against masturbation, nudity, or sex play among children or against the sexual stimulation of children by adults."12

THE CHANGE BEGINS: 1700-1800

Leaving a period that considered youth as something "only time can cure," we note the appearance of a new concept of childhood. The child is now considered to be of psychological interest, and in the 1700's we begin to see a definite change in the approach to childrearing and in the sleeping habits of the people as a whole.

A real propoganda campaign was launched to try to eradicate the age old custom of sleeping several to a bed. Throughout the eighteenth century the advice was repeated that, besides the married couple, it was indecent to go to bed with any other person, especially one of the opposite sex. Parents were urged to teach their children to conceal their bodies from one another.13

In the eighteenth century it was recognized that the child was not ready for life without special and proper treatment and education. The family thus had its birth in becoming the modern concept of "the family," namely an institution in which the child received his first preparation for adulthood and society. The child had taken a central place in his family. Educators and churchmen would from now on be concerned with arguing which views of formal and moral education would be best suited for him.14

The affluent family began to be concerned with privacy. Houses were being built with specific bedrooms, therefore creating places for retreat and isolation.15

A medical textbook of the early 1800's suggests that if possible the nursery, which was the sleeping quarters of the children, not necessarily of only the newborn, should consist of two rooms. This would insure that while one was being used, the other could be ventilated. Pure air was greatly stressed. The nursery should furthermore have a high ceiling, be spacious, perfectly dry, have tight windows, and receive much sunshine.16 It is rather obvious that the advice considered the affluent few only.

BUNDLING

But before the steady decline of co-family sleeping gained full momentum, it enjoyed one final triumph. The custom of bundling came nearest to being a world wide custom, including its practice in America, during the period of 1750-1780.17

The usual definition of bundling is a man and woman lying on the same bed with their clothes on. They may be either conversing or sleeping. They usually were covered with a blanket or quilt.18

The majority of dwellings of the eighteenth century were small, and as in the case of the American settlers, many consisted of only one or two rooms in which the family lived and slept.19

Frequently there were only one or two beds in the house. The scarcity of fuel was to be considered. It became, therefore, only common courtesy to invite a late visitor, who was forced to stay overnight, to sleep with the rest of the family.

Husbands and parents frequently permitted travelers to bundle with their wives and daughters, even if the husband were not at home. Martha Washington mentions quite matter-of-factly in her diary the number of times she slept with strangers while the President was away.20

Since it was rather unpleasant to sit together during the colder part of the year without a fire, it was considered to be proper courtesy that a gentlemen should ask his lady friend to bundle.

This practice was even accepted among the sex-conscious Puritans, who would never have allowed such a practice to prevail had it proven to be a subtle cover-up for sex. Rather, it was stressed time and again that promiscuity and babies were not so much a result of bundling, as of the presence of a sofa or some other suitable place where lovers could retire in private.

"Going to bed" or "sleeping together" has thus not always had the connotation of "having sex" as the implication so frequently is today.

But extra precautions were sometimes taken. In the Pennsylvania Dutch country, any possible over-enthusiasm between maid and lad was securely squelched by mother's tying them each in a separate sack which was then sealed with sealing wax. She then bid the pair a pleasant good night.[21]

Others did not go to such an extreme, but the use of a center board which kept the parties separated was quite common. That this practice was innocently accepted by all visitors unfamiliar with the practice is, of course, to be doubted. Indeed there were those who were quite bewildered when the host suggested that the guest share the family bed.

An example of this attitude may be read in a letter from Lieutenant Anbury, a British officer, who served in America during the Revolutionary War. His letter gives an interesting account of the manners and customs of that period.

The following epistle was dated at Cambridge, New England, November 20, 1777.[22]

The night before we came to this town (Williamstown, Massachusetts) being quartered at a small log hut, I was convinced in how innocent a view the Americans look upon that indelicate custom they call bundling. Though they have remarkable good feather beds, and are extremely neat and clean, still I preferred my hard mattress, and being accustomed to it; this evening, however, owing to the badness of the roads, and the weakness of my mare, my servant had not arrived with my baggage at the time for retirement to rest. There being only two beds in the house, I inquired which I was to sleep in, when the old woman replied, "Mr. Ensign, our Jonathan and I will sleep in this, and our Jemima and you shall sleep in that." I was much astonished at such a proposal and offered to sit up all night, when Jonathan immediately replied, "Oh, la! Mr. Ensign, you won't be the first man our Jemima has bundled with, will it Jemima?" When little Jemima, who, by the by was a very pretty, black-eyed girl of about sixteen or seventeen, answered, "No, Father, not by many, but it will be with the first Brittainer (the name they give to Englishmen). In this dilemma what could I do? The smiling invitation of pretty Jemima, thee, ye lips, the—Lord He' Mercy, where am I going to? But where ever I may be going to, I did not go to bundle with her—in the same room with her father and mother, my kind host and hostess too!

I thought of that. I thought of more besides—to struggle with the passions of nature, to clasp Jemima in my arms—to do

nothing! For if amid all these temptations, the lovely Jemima
had melted into kindness, she had been an outcast from the
world, treated with contempt, abused by violence, and left
perhaps to perish! No, Jemima; I could have endured all this
to have been blest with you but it was too vast a sacrifice,
when you was to be the victim! Suppose how great the test
of virtue must be, or how cold the American constitution,
when the unaccountable custom is in hospitable repute and
perpetual practice.

THE BIG CHANGE: 1800-1900

According to Ryerson, there were probably three kinds of influences which accounted for the drastic change in childrearing
practices which took place during the nineteenth century.

During the latter part of the 1700's, and the first part of the
1800's, there was a strong religious movement which stressed the
importance of personal communion with God and of the Christian
perfection of the individual. "Both of these virtues depended on
self-reliance," writes Ryerson, "a quality it was said best taught by
early independence training."[23] A cry was heard over the country
against bundling. It was in the form of a ballad, "A Poem Against
Bundling; Dedicated to Ye Youth of Both Sexes."[24]

> Hail giddy youth, inclined to mirth
> To guilty amours prone,
> Come blush with me, to think and see
> How shameless you are grown.
>
> 'Tis not amiss to court and kiss,
> Nor friendship do we blame,
> But bundling in, women with men,
> Upon the bed of shame;
>
> And there to lay till break of day,
> And think it is no sin,
> Because a smock and petticoat
> Have chanced to lie between.
>
> etc.

The attitude toward sex and touching which, writes Aries, we would
now consider to be bordering on perversion, became laden with sin.
Earlier and earlier independence was sought in the child. Toilet
training was to begin at between three weeks and six months. The

71

child was expected to be reliably dry at night by the age of three. Punishment was sometimes recommended for failures in cleanliness.

All aspects of sexual behavior in children, e.g. masturbation, sex play among children, etc., were strongly forbidden. Medical writers emphatically disapproved of rocking and singing, handling and cuddling, and the immediate response to the young child's cry. The newborn was still to sleep with his mother, but before he was a year old, he was to be removed from her room to an *unshared* bed.25

Feeding schedules were introduced, and the age for weaning was reduced to approximately nine months. Pacifiers and thumbsucking were explicitly forbidden.

These changes represent a clear trend toward disapproval of dependent behavior. The idea of "teach him early independence or he will be forever dependent" thus had its first stronghold which lasted into this very decade.

In the interesting book *The Unnatural History of the Nanny*, Gathorne-Hardy postulates his view that the English Nanny was also of great influence in changing the childrearing practices during the 1800's. Many of the eating and sleeping behaviors which we expect from children today, were instigated by the Nanny. In many families she was an extremely powerful person, completely taking over the rearing of the children.

Another change which may have had considerable influence on childrearing practices was the change from one family pattern to another. As has been mentioned before, the families were large, including the nuclear family, and the extended family, plus several servants all living in one household. With the industrial revolution, and later the invention of faster public transportation, families began to drift apart geographically. During the 1800's the large family began to be replaced by the nuclear family in which parents and children lived alone together. No longer were aunts and grandmothers available to relieve mother of her childrearing chores. She now had to resume full responsibility. With less help, and therefore less time to spend with each child, independence became a virtue for very practical reasons. The more the child could do for himself, the less time mother had to spend with him, and the more pleased mother was likely to be, especially since she was now the only companion her husband could turn to.

It is interesting to note that Ryerson found no mention of the temper tantrum prior to 1800. "This may mean that people were more tolerant of children's agression or perhaps that children were less aggressive at a time when repression and adult control were not yet characteristic of training in the oral, anal and sexual spheres." This does not necessarily mean, however, that temper tantrums are the primary result of oral, anal and sexual respression.

The increase in scientific knowledge during the eighteenth and nineteenth centuries also had an obvious effect on childrearing advice. Although the germ theory of disease was a much later scientific development, doctors of this period realized that certain illnesses were mysteriously associated with dirt. Once this connection was made, it was reasonable that cleanliness should have assumed a new and crucial significance.26 This presumably led to believing that separate sleeping was more hygienic than co-family sleeping.

In 1893, *Scribner's Magazine* carried what was probably the first twin-bed advertisement to appear in the United States. It read: "Our English cousins are now sleeping in separate beds. The reason is: NEVER BREATHE THE BREATH OF ANOTHER."27

Thus the nineteenth century had set the stage for a type of childrearing which, hopefully, reached its depth during the first half of the twentieth century. Within a hundred years or so, childrearing practices had changed more drastically than perhaps at any other time. Unfortunately these changes did not end in themselves. With natural body drives and needs curtailed, new and other childrearing problems emerged. Problems which had not been present, or had been minor before, now needed special attention. The expert child educators came quickly to the foreground to give their advice on infant nutrition, the child who "clung" to his mother, the child who cried, the child who balked at early weaning, the child who would not go to sleep by himself, the child who grew up into an adult with psychopathological problems.

Women's magazines and books on childrearing gradually took over the role of giving advice which grandmother had occupied until now.28

1900: THE SCIENTIFIC AGE

Around 1900 almost all childbirths still occurred at home with the husband, a midwife, and perhaps other members of the family in attendance. By 1940 that aspect of the family's intimate home experience had also been taken away and most mothers delivered in hospitals. Even the immediate family was now removed.29

As soon as the child was born he was taken out of the hands of his parents and put into the conditioning regimen of society. The emotional intervention by the parents was frowned upon.

The custom of separating mother and child at birth began around this time, presumably because many mothers, drugged at birth, were incapable of taking care of their infants for the first few days post partum. The hospital central nursery was instituted.

With the demonstrable successes of sciences and technology in so many other fields, behavioral psychologists, led by Dr. John Watson, decided to turn their backs on such unmeasurable qualities as motive, emotions, and aspirations. To the behaviorists, the development of the child was shaped entirely by the habits he acquired through contact with his environment.[30]

It was continued to be advised that in order to assure the child's development of "true" independence, mothers should not rock, cuddle or kiss their babies too much, better not at all.

The perplexed mother of the 1920's who no longer was allowed, or perhaps even knew how, to follow her own natural instinct, was now encouraged to turn the pages of a childrearing book which was *the* Dr. Spock book of her time: *The Care and Feeding of Children*, by Dr. Emmett Holt.

One can hardly imagine a more inhumane advice given to a happy mother, to rear a "happy" child. Baby must sleep alone in his own room. He must never be picked up when he is crying unless there seems to be some noticeable cause, because it is necessary for his health that baby cries loud and strong even if he gets red in the face.

He should never be allowed to develop the habit of crying in order to be picked up and rocked, or of sucking or "any other such indulgence."[31]

Discipline is best started in the first few weeks of his life.

And the trusting mothers, intent on doing the "best" for their babies, stood by, themselves frequently crying. One grandmother told me of how she used to sit at the bottom of the stairs, crying, while her little baby was upstairs in his bassinet, crying.

The child had indeed become the major concern of the family, but he was becoming untouchable. He was being moved farther and farther away from his parents.

Bottles took the place of mother's breasts. Cribs took the place of the family bed. Playpens and strollers took the place of his parents' arms. Schedules took the place of mother's intuition. Aloofness took the place, or at least was strongly urged to take the place, of parents' indulging love.

The child was alone in the midst of it all.

Not only was the child removed from the intimacy of the family, but mother, too, was dethroned and replaced by the maidenly figure (not matronly), liberated (without a child in her arms), free-going (replaced by gadgets) woman. It is interesting that a few decades later, Ashley Montagu should write his book *The Natural Superiority of Women.*

During this time the use of single beds became widespread. The idea of separate beds was given by medical advice with the stress on "hygiene." Although the exact type of hygiene desired was rarely mentioned, the factor of communicable diseases may have played an important part.[32] Indeed I have questioned whether there is a connection between medical discoveries of communicable diseases with their stress on minimizing the chance of "catching" some illness from someone else, and the obvious success child psychiatrists *et al* had in convincing parents not to indulge their children. The less one touched, or was touched, the less chance of giving or receiving some horrible sickness.

By this time the myth "It is dangerous to sleep with your baby" had become widespread, and further persuaded mothers to have their babies sleep by themselves. The cause for Sudden Unexplained Infant Deaths used to be termed "overlying," since babies routinely slept with another human being. Now, it is called "crib deaths," because while babies still die of this tragic occurrence, most of these babies sleep, and therefore die, in their cribs. As far as research indicates, there has been no drop in Sudden Unexplained Infant Deaths, even though most Western babies no longer sleep with their mothers. (See chapter "Why Some Parents Hesitate.")

During the 1940's a large array of sleep aids became available, judging from the bedroom business. One could now buy sleep masks, ear stops, knee pillows, sinus masks, tranquilizer bath kits, chin straps, ear warmers, and recordings of soporific music. Some people even put earpieces of stethoscopes in their ears and the receiver on their hearts. The sound of their own steadily beating hearts apparently soothed them and helped them to fall asleep.[33]

Perhaps these gadgets are only subtle substitutes for the warm, soothing, and relaxing companionship which another person could give. Could it be that some of the persons using these gadgets never learned, during their childhood years, to associate the proximity of another person with relaxing?

During this time the "only child" family became popular. Should this be any wonder? Which mother and father would want to have more children, such loveliness, and not be allowed to touch them?

Families were smaller now. Houses were built with three or four bedrooms. Each child could have his own bedroom. Individual bedrooms were no longer the exceptions. They became necessities.

THE RETURN

We move now to the 1950's. Another change is taking place. A few publications concerned with childrearing are suggesting that it is all right for young children to spend some time in their parents' bed.[34] Fathers are beginning to see a glimpse of their children just after they are born. The need for more information about breast-feeding results in the birth of La Leche League. And articles begin to appear suggesting that a crying baby is an unhappy baby who needs comforting.

Some individual natural childbirth classes are given during the 1950's. As word and enthusiasm spread, it is decided to form some type of organization to stimulate communication among isolated efforts. In 1954 the Milwaukee Childbirth Association is formed, and in 1960 the International Childbirth Education Association comes into being at a convention in the same city.

Until mid-1900, Euro-American industrial culture had tended to consider the emotional commitments and care of babies to be mostly a female role. This tendency too, however, was changing, and as father now moved closer and closer to the baby, by being present at his birth, he also seemed to take more demonstrable pride and joy in caring for his offspring. We see fathers pushing strollers, feeding babies, carrying infants on their backs in infant carriers, walking an unhappy, teething baby. As a matter of fact, I fear that some men and women are confused about the role of the father, and believe that he cannot only be a mother substitute at times, but a mother-replacement as well. This shows a sad lack of recognizing and understanding of the great importance of the mother-child relationship.

By 1970 Ashley Montagu's book *Touching: The Human Signifi-*

cance of the Skin had become a best seller. Throughout his book, he speaks highly of co-family sleeping.

Dr. Lee Salk, author of *How to Raise a Human Being* realizes that it is the nature of the parent to take his child to bed with him.

In 1972 a mother writes, "Our last child was born with the assistance of her Daddy. She was nursed in the delivery room and came with us to our room after being briefly checked over in the nursery. Then followed the long, leisurely love-in that I had instinctively wanted with our other five children but never had. This was the first baby I was allowed to hold in my arms for many hours after birth. I know I shall always treasure that beautiful time, a little bit of heaven. During the next two-and-a-half days, Jeanie cried very little, nursed gently and frequently and completely on her own schedule. I had her in my room all day, and on demand at night, which often meant that she slept for several hours in my bed. I was supremely content and happy, and so was our baby."

After mother and baby came home from the hospital, the infant was welcomed into the family bed, which was frequently visited by other children of the family as well.

We seem to be approaching the end or rather the beginning of a full circle. In ancient times, the whole family slept together. Babies were carried around, breastfed and taken care of when in need. They were generally accepted without much further thought. During the early middle ages, the child was still of no particular account in his own right, but during the seventeenth and eighteenth centuries he was beginning to be taken note of as someone who had to be molded. Early independence was stressed. Separation of the members of the family had its beginning.

Although the center of attention by 1900, the child was taken away from the emotional unit, the family. Inventions of every imaginable mother-substitute inundated the parents of the 1930's and '40's. By the 1950's, articles on the big generation gap and the lack of respect youth had for its parents appeared in many a publication.

The 1960's arrive. Young parents are dissatisfied with childbirth and childrearing practices of the previous generation. Prepared childbirth, breastfeeding, a loving, understanding approach to their offspring gain popularity. Family unity is stressed by childrearing publications and groups such as La Leche League.

The Family Bed

Parents are encouraged to stay "in touch" with their children. The young child is slowly returning to the bosom of the family.

SOME ANTHROPOLOGICAL OBSERVATIONS

To be human is to be aware
of the feelings of other human beings.

For some time now, anthropologists, doctors, and others have made intensive studies of societies which have had little or no influence from the modern Western civilization. These are people who live as close to nature as their environment dictates and are not affected by the mechanical world.

It has been observed that the groups, usually non-literate, are not infrequently in remarkably good health, physically and emotionally. Frequent reference is made these days to the excellent physical health of some groups living in remote places, and much effort is made to discover their system of nutrition.[1] It may be fair to assume that these people have a natural wisdom which we in our Western world have lost, forgotten, or overshadowed with a rather know-it-all attitude.

Erick Erickson, the noted psychoanalyst, warns us that we might do well to study the childrearing systems of the non-literate societies. Contrary to our rather arrogant convictions of the unerring ways of our childrearing practices, their methods are far from primitive, and frequently of such integrity that we should envy them, says he.[2]

Whether they are called pre-literate, primitive, or non-literate, these societies are not anachronistic examples of what our own society may have been thousands or hundreds of thousands of years ago.

On the contrary, say Ford and Beach, they may be just as highly "evolved" as European societies. Cultural evolution in different

79

societies has developed in different directions. Instead of specializing in technology and the other trappings which we hold high as representing "civilization," most pre-literate peoples have elaborate cultures of their own. Ford and Beach give as an example the Australian Aranda who have an extremely crude technology. But their kinship system is so elaborate and complicated that it exceeds the comprehension of any European or American unless he is a trained anthropologist.[3]

If the childrearing methods of the past 150 years had resulted in a great improvement over previous methods in rearing happy, emotionally stable people, we might do well to put great stock in it. However, I have found no evidence of such superior results. As a matter of fact, there seems to be more of an indication toward the contrary. The concept of separate sleeping arrangements is of such new vintage that it has not yet had a chance to stand the test of time. The test seems to be on rather shaky grounds. Parents are repeatedly bombarded by yet another book on childrearing, another approach, each claiming to have THE answer. The change is constant. The confusion and frustration persist. It would be of interest, therefore, in the light of the anthropological observations, to relate the types of sleeping arrangements in which people have engaged for thousands of years.

It must again be emphasized, of course, that sleeping together is not going to solve the problems with which we, in our tremendously complex world, are confronted. By reviewing what other peoples do, and by observing the effect on the individual, we may, however, rediscover how best to equip men with an inner strength.

Travelling with his movie camera throughout the world, Hans Hass has shown that many of our human traits, emotional behavior, actions and reactions, and behavior patterns are the same in all men.[4] Sickness and death bring as much sadness and grief to the Bushman as they do to us. Happiness is as much valued by the Arapesh family in New Guinea as in our own family. The need to find comfort in fellow human beings, and have emotional fulfillment, is universal.[5]

In a study by the anthropologist Whiting, it was stated that in forty-eight out of fifty-six societies studied, babies slept with their mothers for at least the first year of life. In twenty-four of these societies the baby slept in between the mother and father.[6] In another crosscultural study by Barry and Paxson, in which 186 different cultures were studied, not one culture reported that mother and father both slept in another room from the baby. In the majority of these cultures, the mother slept with the baby. The father's sleeping proximity varied among the groups. He may have slept in the same bed, or the same room, or sometimes in a different building.[7]

But these statistics are not as vivid as actual anthropological accounts.

In his book *Fear: Contagion and Conquest* Dr. James Moloney, reporting on the Okinawan Indians, writes that from birth until age six, the young children sleep in between their mothers and fathers. The baby always sleeps next to his mother on the same mat. When the pre-schooler reaches school age, he then is moved to another room to sleep with his older brothers and sisters.

Sexual relationship between the parents is not hidden from the children.

The young child enjoys unrestricted breastfeeding and in the event that he is put down, he is immediately picked up and nursed again whenever he begins to cry. Without the restrictions of cumbersome clothing and the taboos on an exposed breast, nursing is much simpler and need not necessarily interfere with what the Okinawan mother is doing.

The Okinawan child is not corporally punished. He is not "toilet trained." He is bowel and bladder educated after he becomes old enough to realize what is expected of him.

The child is not frustrated, and should his mother not be immediately available when he cries, an aunt, grandmother or friend comforts the youngster. The youngster thus receives love, security, tenderness and closeness not only from his immediate family, but from others around him as well. This Dr. Moloney feels is the key to the great inner security the Okinawan person has. He says, "The Okinawan adult not only walks with emotional stability, but with tranquility, with contentment, with pride, with a sense of well being, with love—all of which stems from this basic security he received from his infancy." Dr. Moloney goes so far as to say that after almost a year and a half of close contact with these people, he has never seen more emotionally stable, magnificently integrated adults.[8]

Margaret Mead, in her study of the Balinese child, writes in her account that the youngster spends most of his first few years in the arms or on the back of another human being. Sleeping is enjoyed with the close proximity of other bodies. As adults these people fall quite easily asleep while leaning against other persons. The touch of another person induces relaxation.[9]

The Japanese family sleeps together, and so does the African Bushman. Also, the Korean child sleeps with his mother.[10]

While in the Philippines, Helen Wessel, author of *Natural Child-birth and the Family*, stayed with a doctor, his wife and seven children. The youngest, who was seven, was still sleeping with her parents every night. She slept between them close to the father so the mother could rest, they explained. It was a warm, loving family. Mrs. Wessel was particularly impressed by the fact that the children, most of them teen-aged, *never* quarreled! Mrs. Wessel's daughter, a Peace Corps woman who lived there two years, said she never once heard any of them quarrel. The older children shared rooms and beds, boys with boys, girls with girls.

I note here that a number of American parents have also definitely noticed a reduction in sibling quarreling when the children sleep together.

The emphasis in childrearing by the African community, reports Breetveld, is to teach the child that he is an integral part of the family unit, and to give him a deep-rooted feeling of belonging. They stress a man-to-man rather than a man-to-object relationship. The young child is rarely out of the arms of another person during his first few years of life.[11]

It is believed that the Eskimo's ability to keep such an amiable disposition even though his environment can place him under extremely stressful conditions, is due to the minimum lack of frustration that is placed upon him as a child. There exists a close unity within his family. The very young child is almost constantly carried on his mother's back, and is nursed freely. Since their igloos are quite warm, the Eskimos usually sleep in the nude in close bodily contact with each other.[12] Foreigners who have lived among them have remarked how delightful and happy the children and grown-ups of the far North are, how secure and well integrated the adult personalities. Missionaries who have lived among them to teach them the Christian religion have been known to say that it was not the Eskimos who needed reformation but the white men among them.[13]

Due to Western influence however, many of the natural customs of the above-mentioned societies are, unfortunately, rapidly changing. The customs referred to existed at the time of observation and recording, but do not necessarily exist at the present.

The fascinating difference between the Mundugumor and the Arapesh tribes is given by Margaret Mead in her book *From the South Seas*. The Arapesh people are extremely gentle, loving, trusting. They love children, and a mother will suckle her infant whenever he cries. She does not concern herself with schedules or whether the child may or may not be hungry. The child cries, the mother picks him up, and if he so wants, she nurses him. Through her on-going attempt to soothe the uncomfortable child, he learns first to trust his mother completely, and later his other fellow tribesmen. The child is allowed to wean when he is ready. He sleeps with his parents.

The Mundugumor people are the extreme opposite. They despise the pregnant woman. When a child is born, he is placed in an uncomfortable hard basket. He is nursed only when he simply will not stop crying. His mother stands while she nurses him, and as soon as he stops sucking, if for only a second, the baby is put down. Instead of letting the child wean when he is ready, the security-seeking child is pushed away from his mother. She forces him to wean long before he is ready, but at a time when he can survive on other foods.

These people lack all trust in one another. Till the government outlawed it, they actively practiced head-hunting. They are hateful, distrustful, arrogant. Sexual foreplay is performed with biting and scratching one's partner up to the point of bleeding.[14]

In my reading of anthropological studies I have found that among those societies which seem to produce happy, emotionally stable people, co-family sleeping, unrestricted breastfeeding, and almost constant physical contact with the children in their early years is the custom. (Thus a complete fulfillment of the transition phase, as has been discussed earlier in this book.) This cannot be stressed strongly enough.

I am not suggesting that we copy the patterns of living of the non-literate people. This would be impossible, and irresponsible as we prepare the child for the machine-age society in which we live.

However, a baby's need for breast milk, the best infant nutrition there is; his need for sleeping next to his family members, the best form of security there is; his need to be comforted by another human being, the best comforter there is are needs of children the world over.

A mother's joy in nurturing her child, a father's joy in putting his protective arm around his sleeping child, the parents' need to fulfill their protective instincts are universal needs which will seek to fulfill themselves if freely allowed to do so.

We should not copy other peoples' living customs, but we can learn from them.

The examples I have given are very short and may be inconclusive in themselves. It would require a full book to go into a detailed comparison of the ways of living and their effects on the peoples of other societies and ours.

I hope, however, that my brief account shows its validity and may awaken an interest in studying human relations and learning the art of childrearing of other peoples.

My children, your children, his children or their children, all need our love, fully and unconditionally.

THE INFANT

Bitter are the tears of a child:
  Sweeten them.
Deep are the thoughts of a child:
  Quiet them.
Sharp is the grief of a child:
  Take it from him.
Soft is the heart of a child:
  Do nothing to harden it.
—Lady Pamel Wyndham Glenconner
                "A Child"

"Why do people smile when they see a hospital nursery full of crying babies? One close look at the intensity with which each tiny creature painfully declares his own inborn awareness that something is horribly wrong should wrench our hearts. Deprived of every newborn's birthright to the presence of his mother's warm body and soothing, spontaneous nursing, most hospital-born babies' first experiences are ones of stress rather than warm, loving mothering." (Lucy Cutler) Here is the frustrated, concerned cry of a young mother.

Is there really any bona fide justification for this separation; or is it an antiquated practice, a result of socially and medically oriented events? Is it really necessary that mother and baby be separated after birth, especially in the light of our present-day medical knowledge?

A HOSPITAL BIRTH

Most babies used to be born in the family bed, at home, and slept there till they joined their siblings. Perhaps they spent the first few months in a cradle before sleeping in a bed; nonetheless they were usually near their mothers.[1]

The infant was breastfed shortly after birth, and frequently thereafter whenever he cried.

Today's practice is drastically different. Many hospitals have an arbitrary rule as to how soon after birth a mother "may" have *her* baby. This may be six hours, twelve hours, one day, or even two days.

Frequently a baby is soon after birth quickly shown to the mother, then whisked off to the central nursery (which has been referred to by a prominent doctor as nothing more than a "place for displaced persons"). There his weight, length, physical characteristics and any other traits are recorded. A name and/or number band is placed around his wrist, and then he is put in a bassinet alongside other bassinets.[2]

Gone is the warm, soothing world where no cold, no hunger, no stillness, no loneliness existed. Gone is the heartbeat and the voice so familiar to him. Gone is his mother.

And the mother, who for many months continually felt the presence of that new life, whose arms ache to hold that which her womb no longer carries, whose breasts are full of that rich milk for her baby, is left separated, void and alone. Gone is her child. "Gone at a time," says Montagu, "when a continuing development of the symbiotic relationship is so necessary for the further development of both of them."[3]

Our society tends to ignore or belittle the woman's emotions toward her unique biological functions.[4] The mother is told that her baby is in the nursery so that she can rest and be free from the burden of having to take care of her child. With telephone calls, paperboys, clean-up ladies, and nurses coming and going, how many mothers have really found it restful during their hospital stay? Added to these disturbances is the anxiety of wondering, "Is that *my* baby crying in the nursery?"

Even the makers of paper diapers realize the desire of a mother to hold her infant. But to make it worse, they exploit this feeling

The author and her two-day-old Michelle.

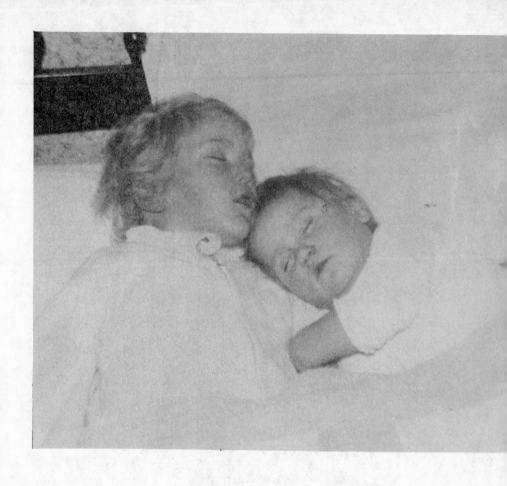

When I took this picture, Peter was four and a half, and Rachelle twenty months. I had crawled out from between them after they had fallen asleep and you see how they gravitated towards each other. They are in the same bed in which they were both born.
—Mother
Toronto, Canada

If we could do it all over again, we would buy a king-size bed at the time of our marriage. —*Mother*
St. Paul, Minnesota

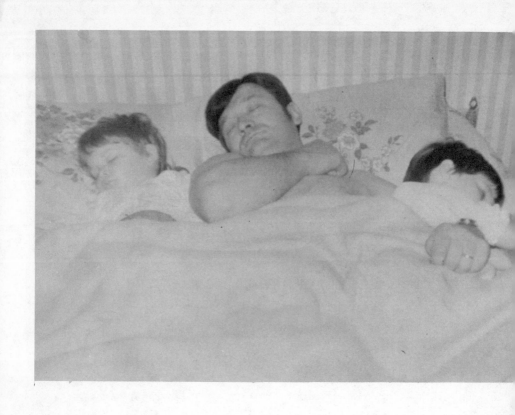

Daddy and his two little daughters.
—Prior Lake, Minnesota

and use it in advertising. One diaper advertisement expressed it:

> A newborn baby spends so little time in his mother's arms. And yet so much time in diapers. Now that he is born you would just love to hold him. But he can't be in your arms all the time you want. . . .

Baby and mother are an emotional unit, and when separated they hurt. Baby cries because he needs his mother. Mother stands anxiously peering at her infant because she needs to give relief, but the nursery glass window separates the two. They both know what is right, but they are told they are wrong.[5]

Much research is now being done in the field of the mother-infant relationship. A growing amount of clinical observations suggests that the degree of contact they enjoy, and the kind of environment in which the mother and child are exposed to each other immediately after delivery, might strongly influence this relationship.[6]

The late Dr. Raymond Albrecht, one of the pioneers in father-participated childbirth, stated, "I'm confident that when the mother and father relate to the baby immediately after birth, somehow or other data is put in his computer. He understands in some way. This is data that will be in the brain forever."[7] This is called imprinting, a word coined by the German naturalist Konrad Lorenz, who made the statement that once imprinting has taken place it cannot be erased nor reversed.[8]

Birth and The Family Journal of 1973 reported in an editorial on the research of Dr. Marshall Klaus. He observed the interpersonal relationship between mothers and their infants during the first few hours after birth and when the children were two years of age. Babies were observed to focus their eyes better in the first hours after birth than in the next few days. They also responded well to the high-pitched voices that mothers often use. The mothers touched and stroked their babies a great deal. After two years, it was noticed that those mothers who had been allowed undisturbed contact with their babies at birth used more gentle clarification and comfort with their toddlers than did the control mothers who were denied early contact with their infants. They also seemed to have greater rapport with their children, concluded the article.

Infants just a few hours old will frequently, when awake and held in someone's arms, stare and stare into the eyes of that person. The imprinting that takes place will be part of the infant forever. Shouldn't this first impression or imprint be as beautiful as possible?

And what face is more beautiful than that of a new mother looking at her own birth gift?

A mother and her newborn babe have every right to be together from birth on. It can only act as a significant contribution toward producing a trusting individual capable of warm, close relationships. Both mother and child have a need for reciprocal stimulation with which one should not interfere. Yet, the greatest interference of all is placed upon them. Separation. The reasons for this separation are now being questioned.

The first interference of the continuance of the mother-child relationship usually comes when the neonate is not allowed to nurse directly following birth. Now some doctors feel that apart from the emotional benefits of placing baby immediately in his mother's arms and allowing him to touch his mother and nurse, it may definitely be better for him and mother physically. Following are some of the benefits which could result from immediate close contact between mother and her newborn baby.

ENGORGEMENT—PLACENTA. There are important benefits of early nursing for the mother. Immediate and frequent nursing drastically reduces the chance of engorgement of the breast. Nursing also stimulates the uterus to contract, which hastens the separation of the placenta from its contact with the uterus. This in turn aids in closing the blood vessels in the part of the uterus to which it was attached, thus reducing the chance of post-delivery hemorrhaging. It also hastens the return of the uterus to the non-pregnant state. Early breastfeeding is used by some doctors to express a reluctant placenta or to check excessive bleeding.[9]

The great beneficial effects of breastfeeding were brought to the attention of a young mother who told me of the following experience she had had.

Several hours after the birth of her second daughter, born at home, her first child playfully fell on her mother's abdomen. Shortly thereafter the mother began to have strong and irregular contractions. They resembled the contractions of the last stages of labor. After some time with no improvement, the midwife who had helped during the delivery was contacted. My friend was advised to start nursing her newborn immediately. Quite soon after she placed the infant to the breast, the contractions became regular.

Mother stayed in bed with her baby nursing and dozing off and on. After a while a clot was expelled, and although tender for some time in the abdominal region, the mother began to feel better.

BABY'S SUCKING REFLEX. In the La Leche League reprint, "On Nursing the Newborn. . .How Soon?" it is stated that the sucking reflex is at its height twenty to thirty minutes after birth. If the infant is not nursed, the reflex diminishes rapidly to reappear again about two days later. On the other hand, if the infant is breastfed soon after birth and frequently thereafter, he takes the breast well and the early physiologic loss of weight is minimized.

Apparently not all babies nurse well immediately following birth. These babies lick the nipple for some time before settling down to nurse. However, more important yet than the baby be encouraged to nurse, is that he should be allowed to touch, smell, and perhaps in other forms unknown to us, establish his contact with his mother. He will then nurse when he is ready.

COLOSTRUM. The first milk, colostrum, is a valuable source of immunity and protection against various diseases and infections. The sooner baby receives this first milk, the better it is for him. No substitutes can provide this protection. The amount of colostrum the baby ingests the first few times he nurses is small, thus the chance of his choking is most unlikely. As a matter of fact, colostrum seems to be an excellent substance to clear and wash down the mucus.[10]

The latest medical research is now also finding that some of the reasons traditionally given by doctors for the separation of mother and her baby are contraindicated.

MUCUS. Dr. Gregory J. White, a La Leche League Medical Advisor, comments that in nineteen years of helping mothers give birth naturally, he has never seen a child have a problem with mucus from early nursing.[11]

T-E FISTULA. Some doctors object to allowing the mother to nurse her infant immediately after delivery because of the possibility that the baby is born with a T-E fistula, an abnormal hole between the windpipe and the esophagus. It is a rare occurrence, about one in 400 births. Dr. James Good, also a La Leche League Medical Advisor, comments that if the doctor suspects a T-E fistula, it would take him no more than thirty seconds to confirm his suspicion. This, Dr. Good writes, can be done right after birth, before the doctor hands the baby to his mother. He feels that in the event a T-E was overlooked, colostrum would be less damaging than if the baby were to drink water and either vomit, or get it into his lungs.[12]

ARTIFICIAL HEATER. Should, however, mother and baby be allowed to have a little nursing time together, no sooner have they established this initial contact than they are faced with another possible separation. Baby usually is, per routine, put into an artificially heated bassinet, or wrapped in aluminum foil, or placed under a heat lamp.

Recent reports seem to indicate, however, that this common practice is unnecessary and may even be bad for the newborn.

There is no evidence that the full term infant of a relatively unmedicated mother will suffer so much heat loss that it would be harmful to him. As a matter of fact, studies from Sweden, Finland, and Switzerland indicate that the results from the slight cooling are good because a cooled brain consumes less oxygen than a warmed brain and there is less danger of oxygen deprivation.[13]

Experiences by Yale-New Haven Hospital in Connecticut and by the late Dr. Raymond Albrecht indicate that when wrapped in a pre-warmed blanket and placed in the arms of his mother, the temperature of the neonate remained stable. The slight cold stress immediately following birth before the temperature stabilizes may act as a stimulus to the onset of respiration in a healthy, vigorous baby.

Likewise, the act of touching is known to stimulate baby's breathing mechanism, and writes Ribble, "enables the whole respiratory process to become organized under the control of his own nervous system."[14]

We may conclude again from this information that in all truth the most logical place for a healthy infant to be, immediately after he is born, is in the waiting arms of his mother, provided she is alert and well. In this event the hospital bed may serve as a temporary family bed. Baby need not leave this bed, not even to be washed. Bathing is another practice which has been subject to controversy the last few decades.

WASHING. We ask again. Is washing the *vernix caseosa,* the cream-like substance with which many newborn babies are covered, really necessary or even advisable? It is believed by some doctors that the *vernix* has beneficial properties in protecting the infant from superficial infections, and acts as an insulating layer against loss of heat and the penetration of too much cold.[15]

During the Second World War, the *vernix* was purposely left on, to be absorbed into the skin. It was a time of scarcity, a time which necessitated the utilization of every resource.

When left on, the *vernix*, like a cold cream, is simply absorbed into the skin, or rubbed off on clothing, usually within one to two hours. If it remains longer, especially in between the creases and folds of the skin, it may be advisable that it be removed.

Any blood that is on the baby's body can be wiped off with a clean cloth. There is no need to bother him with his first bath so soon after he is born.

It is rather ironic that with such concern for heat loss, the baby is first placed in a warmer, then washed, and then, because of possible heat loss during the bath, is placed in the warmer again. This complete procedure is now questioned medically. And while all this fuss is going on, baby could have been peacefully sleeping with his mother and nursing.

Aside from "cleaning him up," bathing the newborn baby as soon as he is born, and daily thereafter while he is in the hospital, is also done for measures of preventing staph infection from sweeping through the hospital nursery. Staph is transmitted by air and hands. The neonate is therefore washed with a strong antibacterial soap.

Readers may remember the Phi-so-Hex drama which took place several years ago. It was discovered that an ingredient in this soap, hexachlorophene, entered the bloodstream through the skin, and caused serious effects in some babies from rashes to convulsions, brain damage, and even death.

John G. Fuller in his book *200,000,000 Guinea Pigs* writes,

Since infants and children are so vulnerable to the chemical, it is hard to understand why it has been almost a universal practice in hospitals to continually bathe newborn babies with it. While Phi-so-Hex is effective as a preventive against staph infections, the question of benefit-to-risk ratio can be sharply questioned except in emergency situations.16

Further on in his book he quoted from an FDA official bulletin, ". . .there is a lack of substantial evidence that hexachlorophene washings by themselves prevent staphylococcal disease or show anti-bacterial activity against gram-negative organisms. Hospitals are known to operate nurseries safely without the use of this product."17

It is ironic, too, that whereas mothers are encouraged to keep their babies in the nursery to curb the spread of infection, the opposite effect has occurred. Infection are more likely to be stubborn and serious when babies are crowded together and bottle-fed in a central nursery.

Fortunately, however, times are changing. More and more hospitals are now attempting to make the birth experience a family affair. They offer rooming-in, a situation in which the mother has her child with her at any time she wishes except during visiting hours, or when situations arise that would prevent her from being with her baby.

The neonate is thus under the constant and watchful eye of his mother. With the reassurance by the hospital staff of her capabilities as a mother, the new couple may spend a few restful, blissful days together. Mother feels complete. Baby feels complete. In fact, together both make a complete unit.

HOME BIRTHS

However, the best place to have a baby when a normal delivery is anticipated, is in the family bed at home. Unfortunately a home birth situation is a service which has sadly lacked empathy from the American medical profession. But there seems to be a trend back to giving birth at home.

Having a baby at home can be safe, especially when the woman has had adequate prenatal care, has been educated to participate actively during parturition, and when there is a knowledgeable mid-wife or birth helper in attendance. Many civilized and technologically advanced countries such as Sweden and the Netherlands have a far lower infant mortality rate than that of the United States. These countries offer as a matter of course a choice between the hospital or home birth with skilled attendance.18

The well researched and excellently written booklet *The Cultural Warping of Childbirth* by Doris Haire, Co-president of the International

Childbirth Education Association, is a source of information well worth reading. It gives a great deal of insight into the reasons why the United States continues to find itself outranked by fourteen other developed countries on the list of infant mortality rates. She points out a number of times that a more natural approach to childbirth both for a home or hospital birth is an important key in lowering the incidence of infant mortality and morbidity.

She emphasizes adequate prenatal education for training in management of labor, minimizing medication and use of obstetrical instruments, and educating the mothers with respect to the hazards involved when these measures, as well as elective induction of labor, are applied. She further stresses the importance of the constant attendance of a skilled midwife and a supportive member of the family during labor and birth, the keeping of separation of mother and infant at a minimum, and greatly encouraging breastfeeding, particularly in the case of a premature birth.

"It may be convenient to blame our relatively poor infant outcome on a lack of facilities or inadequate governmental funding," says Mrs. Haire, "but it is obvious from the research being carried out that we could effect an immediate improvement in infant outcome by changing the pattern of obstetrical care in the United States."[19]

We must not underestimate the sincerity of the medical profession, and the efforts that are made to help those who need physiological help. But neither must we underestimate the wisdom of nature, even at times when we cannot explain it all.

Dr. White of La Leche League said, "I think we are in a little danger in medicine of sometimes spoiling the experiences of healthy people because we are terribly worried about the rare cases."[20]

I feel assured that within the next few decades childbirth will again be regarded in the way it should be: as a family affair. Like the sprays of a fountain, which come from its base, the baby born at home will thus blossom forth from the birthplace of the family, the family bed, rather than being brought into the family from the outside, from the hospital.

There is something special about a baby's being born in the warm, familiar bed at home. It gives a mother a sweet, complete feeling.

PREMATURE BABY. There is a goodly amount of evidence indicating that premature babies do much better when handled and, when possible, nursed by their mothers.

At Stanford University School of Medicine forty-one mothers were encouraged to handle their premature infants at any time of the day or night. There was no increase in the much-feared infections, and no complications of any sort were recorded. The benefits to everyone involved were considerable.[21]

It used to be thought that permature babies did much better on certain formulas than on breast milk since they gained weight faster. It has subsequently been discovered, reports Pryor, that the gain was a result of fluid retention in the tissues. The weight gain on breast milk may at first be slower, but it is a healthy gain.[22]

A La Leche League publication states that breastfed premies "showed better weight gain later on, a better hemoglobin level, and a lower mortality rate."[23]

La Leche League newsletters cite numerous incidents of mothers who have successfully nursed their premature babies. Some doctors even feel that it is possible, indeed desirable, to discharge premies from the hospital much earlier than is usually recommended, especially when they are coming home with a mother prepared to breastfeed her baby. The closeness possible at home is physically and emotionally important to both mother and child, since for all intents and purposes, writes Janov, a premature baby is still a fetus, requiring all the love, warmth, and sensory stimulation provided by the womb.[24] It was concluded in a recent study that early discharge did not increase the risk of morbidity or mortality. (*LLL News*, 1972, p. 28.)

Some mothers of premature babies have instinctively felt that the close contact that the baby received after he came home and joined the family in bed helped to make up for the days or even weeks the infant spent alone. It has also helped Mom make up for the baby-less nights.

There is thus much evidence that in some premature infant cases, separation of mother and child is not only unnecessary but undesirable as well. The foregoing information strengthens the topic of this book: the importance of a close mother-child relationship, beginning as soon after birth as possible, and continuing with baby sleeping with his mother.

HOW BABY RELAXES

It is a human characteristic to be sociable and to have the urge to cuddle. This is very strong in young children, especially when they are falling asleep. They seek to recreate the snug, comfortable, warm, secure feeling of life *in utero*.[25]

Anna Freud has commented that children have more difficulty in falling asleep when separated from their mothers. This may not be the case if a child feels comfortable with a favorite article which serves as a mother substitute. But a breastfeeding mother knows that even though she may have nursed her child an hour before bedtime, he wants to nurse again as a means of relaxing and drifting off to sleep.

Nursing mothers may also notice that their breasts, especially the left breast, pulsate gently with the beating of their hearts. The nursing baby will thus actually feel the heart beat which he heard and felt before he was born. How much closer could a child get to that life before birth? Breastfeeding has such a soothing effect on the child. Breastfeeding means "to comfort," whether the baby experiences hunger, pain, tension, or loneliness, a need to suck, to feel, or to touch. Breastfeeding means more than feeding at the breast.

Should we have to "prove" that babies are more relaxed and better off when they are with their mothers? Dr. Lee Salk devised a machine which reproduced the human heart beat. Newborn babies, hearing this, slept better, were happier and even gained weight faster, reports Salk, than those infants who spent their days in the customary hospital nursery.[26]

It is incredible that the importance of hearing the mother's heart beat could have been so readily accepted and used by dog owners, but ignored until recently for human babies. Most of us know that when a puppy has been taken away from its mother, a loud clock, wrapped in a towel, as a surrogate for his mother, will quiet down the lonesome pup. But modern science has finally caught up with the dog owners. Mothers can now buy tapes and phonograph records which they can play for their lonesome babes while they busy themselves with other things. The recordings play sounds from "a mother's womb, her heart, her main artery, and her veins," and, as one record claims, "familiar music from the baby's environment." It is to be desperately hoped that only a few parents will fall for this mechanical, degrading trap. Which adult would passively accept a tape recorded message, "I love you," sent by a loved one who chooses not to deliver his adoration in person?

After learning about all the "fabulous" inventions which serve as mother substitutes, are supposedly so much "like mother," but unfortunately bring with them their inevitable breakdowns, one doctor exclaimed, "Eureka! Why don't we use mother?"

Let's quickly go back to things that speak of love. Some young babies, after falling asleep in their mother's arms, wake up the instant they are put down. As a solution to this problem, many a mother lies down with the child until he has fallen asleep. And then it is so easy to slip away from him without his awakening. Lying down with the child can, therefore, be relaxing for mother as well as for the youngster.

One of the most tender stories that was related to me told of a mother and her six-week-old infant. The baby had fallen asleep in his mother's arms, and was then laid on the large bed of his parents. Mother, not wanting to disturb the child, lay down a few feet away from the little one, and also fell asleep. When she awoke, she found her baby curled up snugly against her. While mother was asleep, the infant evidently maneuvered himself over to her, where he felt he belonged.

CRYING

Whether during the day or at night, parents need not be afraid to pick up their child as soon as he starts to cry. We've heard a lot about spoiling little babies by picking them up the minute they cry, or how normal it is for them to cry it out for a while, or how healthy crying is for the young infant.

"The truth is," says Salk, "that by picking him up we are teaching him that someone responds to his needs, whether it is the need for physical sensation or for food."[27]

Anthropologists have repeatedly reported that there is one striking dissimilarity between babies in the Western world, and babies in the pre-literate world. In the latter, babies are seldom heard to cry, and if they do, they are usually immediately picked up and nursed, or soothed in some other way. I need not comment on the crying of the Western baby. One hears it everywhere, and for longer than a few minutes.

A popular American book on child care advises letting baby cry in his crib for fifteen to thirty minutes if he has to, since some children fall asleep faster this way.[28]

In the early 1950's a study of infants was made in an American nursery. Observers recording infants' behavior twenty-four hours a day, indicated that the average infant cried for almost two hours daily![29]

I was told recently by a mother who had just delivered her baby in a hospital that she had overheard one nurse say to another, "We will have to put that one crying baby in the 'Naughty Baby Room.' He keeps waking the other babies up with his screaming and hollering."

The almost unfailing action with which animal mothers respond to their infants' cries, i.e. immediately going to and touching the infant, should perhaps further give us insight into the importance of the immediate physical response to the cry. Indeed, reports Bowlby, it should be of serious concern to us that in our "advanced" and "civilized" society we should act in a way so utterly against this very basic natural behavior; behavior which is present among most pre-literate people and animals.[30]

"There is no harm in a child crying; the harm is done if his cries are not answered," says Dr. Salk.[31]

Crying is the infant's first form of social communication because it calls for a response by another person. He is sounding a distress signal to let others know he is in need of something.

Perhaps the feeling of utter desperation and loneliness that an infant who is left to cry must have may be best imagined by those who have had the misfortune of being totally dependent on others, such as during a hospital stay. When no one comes with a soothing word, a drink of water, a pain-relieving medicine, or some other response to a call, one tends to become bitter and lose faith in the people around him. If this happens once, the incident is most likely soon forgotten. But should this happen frequently, it would be a rare person who would not be adversely affected.

It is rather interesting that the interpretation of a baby's cry as a deliberate means to wrap us around his little finger and dominate us has been believed by so many people. Several mothers have told me that they loved holding their babies so much they could hardly wait for their infants to begin crying, just so they could pick them up. In this light the crying takes on a totally different, and I believe more realistic hue. The first interpretation shows a basic fear of the child; the second gives him credit for being a basically

97

cooperating human being.

Desmond Morris in his book *Intimate Behavior* states that it is difficult to comprehend the warped tradition which says that it is better to leave a small baby to cry so that he does not "get the better of you."[32]

Instead of encouraging mothers to meet the baby's emotional needs, one doctor advocates using the "I'll-make-you-stop-crying" method. A mother of a nine-month-old baby who cried a great deal and was in constant need of his mother's presence, called her doctor for advice. He told her to ignore the child for three days, and not to pay special attention to him other than at feeding and bath times. If after three days the youngster did not stop crying and clinging, he would hospitalize the baby for three to four days. "This has always done the trick," said the doctor. (She did not follow his advice.)

There is an old Yiddish proverb which says, "Small children disturb your sleep, big children your life." Dr. Herbert Ratner elaborated on this proverb in his Keynote address to the 1964 La Leche League International Convention.

If we don't lose sleep over our children when they are young, we will lose sleep over them when they are old. Though it is easy to ignore an infant—he is a little thing, you can close the door on him, it seems to you to be a private matter since there are no witnesses around—just remember that it is not going to be as easy to ignore the cries of an older child, a child who gets into trouble with the law, a child who is a juvenile delinquent. Now it becomes a public matter, and you have a responsibility. So just remember in the middle of the night when you get up, not too joyously, to take care of the needs of your infant, that this is the natural time to have your sleep disturbed. It is going to be awfully grievous when, as a result of not permitting your sleep to be disturbed when your babies need you, your sleep is going to be disturbed in many more complicated ways when the child grows older.

Should we not rear children in the happiest way possible? They at times encounter so much unhappiness. Why add to it? The next time a baby or child cries, ask yourself, is this crying really necessary? Could it be avoided—with a little love for instance?

Parents who have chosen to have the child begin the night in a crib or bed other than theirs, ought therefore to be assured that they should feel no hesitancy in immediately rising and getting the child as soon as they are awakened by his crying or calling. The opposite of love is not hatred, it is indifference says Montagu. When a child's cry does not arouse immediate reaction from a person, how else can he interpret it than as not caring?

SOLUTIONS TO CRYING

Babies who still cry even after their mothers have "tried everything," can cause a bit of distress, especially during the night. The following suggestions as to the causes of and possible solutions to the problem of crying may be helpful.

A baby may become more fussy and demanding if he senses a feeling of resentment in the mother. Try, therefore, to feel enjoyment in those quiet night times together—they won't last forever. It would also help not to look at the clock when he awakens. Take off your watch. It is amazing how much the knowledge of the number of times and at what hours one was awakened can influence one's disposition.

We might consider it our right to have a good night's sleep. But, as Dr. White of the La Leche League Advisory Board, father of eleven children said:

A lot of people are so square as to think they're entitled to a night's sleep. Nobody is entitled to a full night's sleep, whether a parent or not, if someone needs her or him.

Let your baby know that he is loved unconditionally, that you welcome him into your arms at any time.

With kind permission of Jean Perkins, La Leche League Counselor, I have taken the following excerpts from her reprint "Possible Causes of Crying and Frequent Nighttime Nursings."*

Baby could be hungry.
Does he need burping?

---

*Some of these suggestions apply more directly to either daytime crying, or to the baby who sleeps by himself. I have purposely left those suggestions in, however, since I assume that many a mother would welcome the mention of many possible solutions to the crying of young children.

99

He may feel too warm or too cold.

His diaper may need changing.

He may feel tired.

Perhaps he has been over stimulated by light or noise.

Is he bored? Being close to mother or having bright things to watch can help.

Has he been insecurely or roughly handled?

Can you observe any signs of illness?

He may be troubled by too much handling. (But not as likely as from too little.)

Have there been great changes in his routine or people who have handled him?

Personality plays a part—some babies just seem to cry more than others.

He may need additional motion or rocking.

He may need more consistent routine, or fewer outings until he is more mature.

Baby may be noticing tension or insecurity in his mother—or problems or conflicts in the home.

Teething may cause fussiness even before teeth appear above the gums.

His sleeping or lying position may need changing.

Especially sensitive babies may need to have their nursing routine adapted to them. (Example: only one breast per feeding.)

He may be disturbed by substances eaten by the mother: drugs, allergens, foods, etc.

Don't feel like a failure if baby cries, but don't let him cry alone. Keep looking for other possible reasons why he is in distress.[33]

Some mothers felt that cupping their hand over the tiny infant's head, and applying a slight pressure would stop baby's crying. Another mother found that gently blowing on baby's head would quiet him down.

Dr. Niles Newton feels that perhaps one cause for crying may be baby's missing the womb. In her reprint, "When Baby's Crying Becomes Trying," she comments that some mothers, especially breastfeeding mothers, "go back to the ways of their great-great-grandmothers when faced with a fussy baby at night." She makes reference to old medical text books which emphasize the need for the infant to be comforted by sleeping with his mother.

She recommends:

If the bed seems a bit crowded, consider a king-size bed. Some couples prefer to have a mattress on the floor for mother and baby while they sleep and nurse. When the baby goes to sleep, he is left on the mattress and mother goes back to bed with her husband.

If a baby or child is especially restless during an illness, father could perhaps sleep elsewhere for the night. Or mother and child could rest in another room so as not to disturb other members of the family. I do believe that even though both parents are responsible for rearing the children, it is only fair that father, usually the breadwinner, gets his sleep, when possible. This certainly does not mean that he should not help out when needed. At times his reassuring voice or touch can work wonders, especially in the middle of the night.

What is crying? Desmond Morris writes, "crying says 'come here,' and smiling says 'please stay.' "[34]

MOTHER AND BABY MAY DREAM IN UNISON

Breastfeeding mothers may have noticed that not infrequently they will awaken in the middle of the night shortly *before* their baby begins to whimper. Results of recent research suggest, according to an article in an LLLI publication, that a nursing mother may awaken in anticipation of her child's cry because she and her infant dream in unison. It is suspected that the hormone prolactin may be the key to this mysterious link. This lasts for only as long as breastfeeding is continued. With bottlefed infants and their mothers this will last only for about two weeks. After that, mother and child have completely different and unequal sleep cycles.[35]

Research further indicates that the very deep sleep periods are extremely important and essential for a restful sleep and a feeling of well being during waking hours. When the deep sleep periods are repeatedly interrupted, the person becomes groggy, irritable, and depressed during the day.[36]

Since a mother and her nursing infant seem to have equal sleep periods, mother, also, sleeps during her deep sleep periods (if no other interruptions awaken her). Should her baby awaken, this would most likely be during a lighter sleep. Is this therefore another reason that nursing mothers do not find nighttime interruptions as objectionable and are not quite as affected by them as bottlefeeding mothers? A bottlefed baby may awaken at a time when his mother is in a deep sleep period.

CHILD'S SLEEPING POSITION

Several books on child care go quite some length into the sleeping position of the newborn. Should he be on his front, back, or side? Then which side? For how long?

These problems are also solved when baby sleeps with his mother, especially the breastfeeding baby. While nursing, whether awake or asleep, the infant lies on his side and since the mother may also fall asleep, this position is held until the baby lets go of the nipple. He then may move to his back, stomach, or other side. With the next feeding, the mother quite naturally nurses him on the other side, and so during the course of the night, baby may sleep on all four sides. The chances of his developing a deformed head from lying in one position too long and too frequently are automatically nullified.

Some parents have noticed an interesting difference in the sleeping positions of their babies. When the child sleeps alone he seems more apt to curl up or sleep on his stomach. When he is in bed with others, he seems to prefer his side, or back with his arms extended.

Several parents have told me how soothing they have found it for baby to sleep on Mama's or Papa's chest. A mother wrote, "At first if baby didn't want to nurse but was restless, I would just put her on my bare chest and she'd sleep."

BABY AWAKE AT NIGHT

At times we hear of the little baby who has his days and nights all mixed up. When I have talked with mothers of such babies, the circumstances are not infrequently the same. Baby goes to sleep for his morning nap. He is put down and sleeps for three or four hours. Then he awakens, eats, looks around a bit, and then takes another long nap. Mother is delighted with all the free time that she has while baby is sleeping. She hesitates in picking baby up since he sleeps so nicely. Then nighttime comes around. Everyone is ready for sleep, except baby.

I feel that if baby is carried around more during the day, even when he is dozing, he would receive enough stimulation to keep him more awake and he would consequently sleep at night.

The baby who is carried a lot by his mother, and who takes naps on his mother's person, is known to sleep well almost anywhere. These babies need no crib to nap. As long as they are close to someone they will sleep when tired. They have learned to associate the human body with comfort, warmth, and a state of relaxation which easily lulls them to sleep when they are tired. Carrying an infant even while he is napping is really not depriving him horribly of some necessary human need, which is, supposedly, to lie flat in bed while sleeping. However, such was apparently the feeling of a concerned lady who saw a child of eight months peacefully sleeping on his mother's lap. "That poor child," she remarked disgustedly to her friend. "He should be in his crib."

Sleeping on a person may at one time have been the usual way human infants took their naps. This still happens among peoples who take their babies wherever they go. Many readers may have seen pictures of Oriental women working in the fields, shopping at a market place, or working in a factory, while their babies were strapped to their backs in a sling, peacefully sleeping.

But we would not have to cross the ocean for examples. Each year we see more and more mothers and fathers out walking or biking or shopping with their little ones on their backs in a back carrier, or in front with a specially designed baby sling. Frequently these babies are fast asleep. One man even remarked: "Those carriers must be the most fantastic invention ever made. I have never yet seen a baby cry when he is carried that way. Whatever did mothers do without them?"

As tempting as it is to let sleeping baby sleep during the day, it may be of actual benefit to all if he is picked up and held a lot during these hours.

The baby who sleeps with a pacifier or his thumb in his mouth may sleep longer than he would if he were totally breastfed. In the latter case he would awaken to seek his mother.

Sometimes babies are awake during the night due to causes other than sleeplessness, e.g. colic or teething. They are awake no matter how much or how little sleep they had during the day.

Babies are like adults. Some are naturally "owls" and some are naturally "larks." And with a few babies no matter what their mothers do, they seem to insist on being awake during the night and sleeping during the day.

Perhaps the most important thing to remember in a situation such as this is that *it will not last forever.*

WHEN WILL MY BABY SLEEP THROUGH THE NIGHT?

(from the reprint by Jane Wolfe, LLL Counselor)

This is a common question.   The real issue, of course is not "when will the baby sleep throught the night?" but "when will I be able to sleep through the night?" Getting this distinction straightened out is important.   Certainly an infant sleeping sixteen to twenty hours a day, more or less, is not the one who is going to be upset because he wakes up a couple of times when the sun is shining in China. The fact that you are crawling the walls in despair might cause him some concern; but as far as getting the anxieties because he's not resting enough—that's no problem.

What's wrong is not the baby's waking up, but our getting upset about it and feeling tired because of it.   We've been brainwashed by some great, tyrannical, mysterious sleep lobby (ASA - American Sleep Association, AMM - American Mattress Makers, PSPQ - Parents Seeking Peach and Quiet: these are the charter members of the sleep lobby) into thinking that unless we have eight to nine hours of uninterrupted sleep nightly, we will at the end of a few desperate days be on the brink of total mental and physical collapse. This isn't true.   Huge hunks of sleep are nice and occasionally called for, but as a steady diet they aren't necessary; and moderate-plus-small doses of sleep, plus the utilization of a few conscious relaxation techniques, will do just as well, perhaps better.

Up until Small arrived on the scene, there was no particular need to get out from under the sleep lobby's dictates.   But he arrived, and with his intense infant needs, calls for you with all body and soul. Four a.m. Last time you heard from him was two a.m.

"What will it be?"

1. Cereal—(a) which might not work; (b) to which he may be allergic; (c) which he certainly doesn't need; and (d) isn't what he's calling for anyway?
2. Let him cry it out, which—(a) will exhaust him; (b) will let him get the anxious drift that when he needs you he might not be able to count on you to come; and (c) will guarantee

you no sleep at all the rest of the night?

3. (a) get up; (b) stomp into his room; (c) resentfully get him out of bed; (d) satisfy his immediate needs, but (e) basically transfer your tension to him so that either he (1) can't get back to sleep at all (2) not for very long, in which case you'll be back again at five-thirty a.m.?

4. Free yourself from the terrible tyranny of the eight-to-nine-hour-a-whack sleep syndrome so that you can, with cheerful acceptance, meet your tiny one's needs at any hour, and at the same time feel happily rested and energetic?

"How to Accomplish No. 4"

1. Truly believe there is an alternative to your previous in-a-rut thinking about sleep and that that alternative is worth pursuing for the sake of you, your baby, your husband, and whoever else in your family is suffering from your present conflict (baby's needs vs. your sleep).

2. Realize that changes in life style, and this is one of them, are part of the whole business of becoming and being a mother; that they are part of the pattern of the great new personal growth that is taking place as you are assuming the wonderful new responsibilities that come with the birth and growth of a child: Finding new ways of rest that allow you to meet a baby's needs with enthusiasm at any hour is an exciting, not a depressing prospect.

3. Catch-up sleep, if you need it, isn't really that hard to come by. Saturdays and/or Sundays, Papas are very good at taking baby on outings; and that's another couple of hours in the bag without even working.

4. Don't forget bringing the baby to bed with you. This often accomplishes two ends on one mattress. Baby cud es and eats. you ZZZZZ away, and no one is the more awake fo it.

5. Remember to rest when the baby rests rather than mopping and going. The time in the early weeks, when baby spends most of his time asleep, is the best time for learning the art of smaller-hunk sleeping. Try resting when junior does. If you don't get to sleep every time at least you'll be learning to relax, and probably will sleep some of the time.

* * *

According to Luce and Segal, co-authors of the two books *Sleep* and *Insomnia*, many people are getting more sleep than they think they are.

It is evidently difficult to estimate how much sleep one is actually getting. Unless one can see his EEG tracings, say Luce and Segal, he doesn't really know for sure. But the lack of sleep is probably overestimated. One may have dozed off half a dozen times without knowing it. It should be some satisfaction to know, however, that the discomfort, due to lack of sleep, is seldom as disastrous as one may think.[37]

A mother may strive to have her little one sleep through the night, but there is little she can do to attain this goal. Through-the-night sleeping appears to need a certain maturation of the brain. It is not a matter of love, nor of the baby's intelligence. Sleep is not a skill to be learned, and the baby will go at his own pace of development.[38]

Studies also show that the giving of solids has little or no effect on the child's sleeping through the night. Some babies begin sleeping through the night at seven days. Others are four years old before they sleep through in one stretch. Some babies, after sleeping continually during the night for several months or even years, may suddenly begin to awaken at night. They may wake up once or twice for several days or months before sleeping through the night again. Frequently we do not know what causes the change. But this we do know: if they call us, they need us.

BREASTFEEDING WHILE LYING DOWN

Most nursing mothers find lying down with an infant to be very relaxing. With a first time baby, it might take a few trials to find the most comfortable position, but this usually does not take long at all. It is important to remember that whichever position you and your baby find most comfortable is the one best for you both.

La Leche League's manual *The Womanly Art of Breastfeeding* gives this suggestion when first lying down with your baby:

If you are going to nurse your baby on the right side, lie down on that side, put your right arm up over the baby's head or under it, whichever is more comfortable for you. With the left arm, bring the baby toward you *till his cheek is touching your breast,* with the nipple next to his mouth. He will turn his head toward it, for this is the way he is built, and open his mouth. When he does, pull him a bit closer, just enough so he can get the nipple into his mouth and suck. For nursing on the left side, reverse all this. If you pull his legs close to you, it angles his body enough to keep his nose free. This keeps him warm and cozy besides.39

When ready to nurse baby on the other side, gently hug baby against your body, roll over, and settle down on the other side. You can also do this while he is still nursing.

It might be comfortable in the beginning to tuck a pillow behind your back. Once you become really adapted to nursing lying down, you could try "overlapping." This is nursing the baby with the left breast, but remaining on your right side. It is not quite as comfortable, but it can be very convenient.

It is always our intention to provide as safe an environment as possible for our children. Nevertheless, dangers lurk everywhere. The following letter was taken from the La Leche League publication *Leaven*, November, 1974.

I have appreciated the recent warning about how little ones can swallow pins, zipper pulls, etc. but thought, "I'm careful, that will never happen to me." One never can tell. . . .Last night around 3:00 a.m. I brought the baby into bed with us to nurse, unbuttoned my pretty nightie and untied the shoestring bow at the top, put her to the breast and promptly fell back to sleep. When I awoke this morning and rolled over, I noticed the tie was caught and pulled gently to free it. When it wouldn't come loose I looked to see what it was cuaght on and was horrified to see it was wrapped twice around the baby's neck, loosely but nonetheless firm. I gently freed it and as I hugged Sarah close to me shuddered to think what combinations of her movements or mine might have produced a tragedy. As I cut the bow off the nightie this morning I thought how many other mothers might have nighties with long bows or shoestring ties. I know I have another gown that is perfect for nursing for it ties over each shoulder, but, when undone, those ties are about twelve inches long and equally as dangerous as last night's nightdress.

I am surprised I didn't consider the danger of those ties for I did think of the danger of the venetian blind cord (actually a perfect hangman's loop) on the window near her bed, and had taken great care to hook it up where Sarah couldn't reach it. Ceiling-to-floor curtain cords also present a similar danger to creepers.

SLEEPING ARRANGEMENTS

Because our beds are usually too small and too high, and the bedroom too crowded with the regular bedroom furniture, most families who turn to family sleeping, have had to improvise in making accommodations for the whole family to sleep together. The following solutions were related by parents through the questionnaires.

"When baby gets big enough to roll out of bed we have to push furniture against the open end as a safety measure. Some interior decorators would cringe. I have had guests who think it is an awful way to sleep and live. Their criticism falls on deaf ears. In a few short years all the children will be grown and gone and we can have a wall-to-wall Better Homes and Gardens bedroom then."

Some parents have been fortunate to be able to buy a larger bed or have resorted to placing two twin-sized beds together. A father wrote his solution in an amusing poem.

Father's Lib (at 2:00 a.m.)
by
Wally Bennett
Oh, how nice it would be,
If other Dads could be like me.
While they're up and bottles pouring,
I'm in bed soundly snoring!
—That is, of course, if there is room.

At 1 a.m. Baby pops in,
Then a toddler kicks me in the shin.
Mommy's hanging off the edge,
Sister's on the other ledge.
Poor Dad can't move or do a thing—
Except to buy a SUPER KING![40]

Pillows and blankets or foam rubber pads around a low bed have served as safety measures until the baby could crawl from the bed by himself. And some parents have resorted to the most logical solution, namely wall-to-wall bed made just from mattresses.

But as logical as it might seem, it may not always be the most practical, or even necessary. To enlarge the parents' bed, an adjustable crib can be placed right next to the big bed, set to the height of the bed. Or a picnic bench can be placed between the bed and the wall, built up with blankets to the height of the master bed. The slight space between can be covered with a blanket or bed pad. Or two chairs, facing each other, with one board bridging the seats, will solve the problem.

If there is room enough, another bed can be placed in the parents' room, either next to it, on the foot end, or somewhere else in the room. A side rail is another solution. Or place the bed in a corner against the wall, and have children sleep between Mom and the wall.

A mattress or sleeping bag on the floor next to the big bed has also been a good solution. Watch out for drafts, though.

One mother wrote, "My husband built a sleeping platform for us. It is seven feet long and eight feet wide, and two inches off the floor. The size was deliberately planned for three, since we realized that neither baby nor ourselves would welcome a separation. Baby has been with us all this time. We took her crib down after a few months and have resolved never to use it again."

The urine, bowel movement or vomit of a totally breastfed baby does not smell unpleasant. This is undoubtedly another reason why breastfeeding mothers do not hesitate to take their babies into bed with them. Should the baby or young child wet the bed, a towel placed under him will quickly give him a dry place to sleep again. Keep a towel handy under your pillow for such emergencies. A rubberized flannel sheet beneath the bedsheet prevents the mattress from getting wet. Putting a double diaper on baby will also help prevent wet sheets.

Have a small supply of toys on hand, even for the three to six month old. This can be another sleep saver for those times when the little one decides to wake up before the rest of the family wants to get up. Many babies are most content to lie between their parents, play or nurse or just look around. They might even fall asleep again for a short while.

For naps, the infant may be safest in that time-honored little bed, the cradle. It is a snug and secure place, nice to lull the baby to sleep. The gentle back and forth motion of the cradle simulates the mother's breathing and walking. A buggy in the living room will serve the same purpose.

But no matter how pretty or cozy or handy his bed, it should only serve as a temporary resting place. It is in the arms of his mother that a baby will grow the most. Just remember that children are very adaptable and will adjust to almost any sleeping condition. They do not necessarily need a large, smooth bed. If they are happy and relaxed they will sleep almost any place.

If a problem arises for which no immediate solution can be found or which seems momentarily irritating, it is important not to think, "If he had been in his own bed. . ." because this leads to resentment. Rather, accept the fact that he sleeps in your bed, and that solutions have to be found from that point.

Unfortunately, ours is a society in which we are conditioned to find instant solutions to unpleasant situations. Instant weight-reduction foods, pills, menus, gadgets are big sellers these days. (It says so on the package!) We can buy instant meals from breakfast to frozen dinners. We have instant pain relievers. "Instant Possession, Pay Later," blares the advertisement. Babysitters and separate bedrooms instantly relieve us from our children.

When we are then faced with a problem concerning our children for which there is no instant solution, we panic. We are pressured into finding an immediate answer, instead of receiving encouragement, understanding and support for what we are going through and are doing to make the best of the situation.

CONCLUSION

"Only as we discover and assimilate the truth about nature," wrote Lorenz, "shall we be able to undertake the apparently contradictory but essential task of reestablishing our unity with nature and at the same time maintaining our transcendence over nature."[41]

Society has moved the infant away from his mother at a time when, in normal cases, separation is totally contraindicated. Mother and Babe need each other, and every effort should be made to meet this natural necessity. Nature is not perfect. And we can benefit from the learnings of men. However, man must not find himself so confident that he apparently chooses to ignore the natural emotions of the new couple. These emotions must be respected and protected, for only then can a mother and her child grow.

THE CHILD PAST INFANCY

The child's sob in the silence curses deeper
Than the strong man in his wrath.
                    —Elizabeth B. Browning
                    "The cry of the children"

It is almost unanimously agreed that it is quite common for the young child to feel lonesome or frightened at night. Parents are advised, therefore, to leave a light on in the child's room or in the hallway, and to be sure he has his favorite blanket or toy.

"But the real reason for his loneliness," contends Montagu, "the primary need for the child to have close and warm contact with another person's body, is totally disregarded."[1]

Children are rather adaptable creatures, however. Placed in single beds, isolated in separate bedrooms, they snuggle up to their toys.[2] Dolls are now available which talk to the child, the way he would like his mommy to talk to him. Parents are urged to buy the doll whose advertisement may read:

When you're two and a half and you've just been tucked into bed, don't you wish that falling asleep weren't so lonesome? That's what this doll is for. It's so nice when someone stays with you to keep you company until you fall asleep. And you couldn't hope to find a softer sleepmate than this doll. It lulls her "mommy" to sleep with phrases like, "Mommy, kiss me goodnight." "Mommy, hug me tight." "Mommy, I love you."

BEDTIME RITUALS

Owing to the misconception that it is healthy for children to sleep, rest and play alone, children are forced to sleep by themselves instead of in the parental bed. "This neglect of natural needs," says Anna Freud, "is the first break in the smooth functioning of the processes of need and drive fulfillment." As a result, mothers seek advice for their children who have sleep difficulties.

Montagu describes these difficulties well: "In our Western culture," he writes, "one constantly encounters the phenomenon of children begging their mothers to lie by their side or at least to stay with them until they fall asleep." But mothers tend to discourage these requests. The endless calls of the child for the presence of the mother, for an open door, a drink of water, a light, a story, to be tucked in and so on, are all symptoms which Montagu regards as the child's need for that primary object, his mother, to whom he can securely relate. When mother's presence is lacking, the child resorts to other means of falling asleep. A cuddly toy, a pet one can take to bed, soft materials, and autoerotic activities such as thumb sucking, rocking, and masturbation, are means to which the child may resort in his drive for security. "When these objects are given up," continues Montagu, "a new wave of difficulties in falling asleep may develop."3

It is not that he should be denied a doll or teddy bear in bed with him, but he should have his Mama or Papa also.

After the child has drifted off to sleep, the parent certainly need not stay until he himself is ready to go to bed. It may well be advised though, to remain with the youngster for a few minutes after he seems to have fallen asleep, to make sure he is, indeed, sound asleep.

Children may still ask for water, a story, or one more bathroom visit. Perhaps the child is not tired enough and is therefore bored with being in bed even though a parent is with him. A drink of water can be given. Just make it a routine to have a glass of water by the bed. I, personally, find it unjust to deny water to a thirsty child. Thirst is a very uncomfortable feeling. If one of my children did indeed drink water, and I could see the possibility of bed wetting, I would make sure to pick her up and put her on the toilet a few hours after she had gone to sleep. I did this quite frequently when my children were small. This procedure never awakened them enough to cause them difficulty in falling asleep again. And they usually slept right through the interruption. A story before sleep is a relaxing favorite bedroom ritual of children and adults alike. The difference lies in the motive behind asking for a story, a glass of water, etc.

What of the time that one spends lying down with his children until they have fallen asleep? This may sometimes take as long as forty-five minutes. Is this time wasted? We can readily think of many things we could be doing. Is there anything to be gained? Yes, there is. For the child it means a happy, secure feeling of love and a relaxing way to fall asleep. For the parent it means a chance for growing, maturing in the ability to freely give himself to those who need him, to place his immediate wants and needs second to someone else's wants and needs. This is one of the most noble acts in life.

If it takes much longer for the child to fall asleep, perhaps he may yet be a little bit hungry. Some nutritious snack, an apple, some yogurt, a piece of carrot, some nuts, just before his teeth are brushed may help. He may be overstimulated and may not have had a chance to relax. Or he may not have had enough play and fresh air and sun during the day.

The ultraviolet rays that are contained in outdoor sunlight have far-reaching effects on the body. They lower blood pressure, increase metabolism and stimulate growth. They change the depth of respiration so profoundly that the effect may last for hours.[4]

Mothers with busy schedules, air-conditioned houses in the summer, a fear of catching a cold in the winter, make outdoor play at times almost a forgotten thing.

And don't forget the weather. It has forceful influences on people, and has a lot to do with the way a person acts and feels. Although children may not seem to be bothered as much as adults by extremes of temperatures and humidity, these conditions, nevertheless, may affect their ability to fall asleep. Also, the barometric pressure has an influence on the way we behave and feel.[5]

Difficulty in falling asleep may be due to a long, late nap. Even a short nap late in the afternoon may refresh him so much that he is not sleepy at the regular bedtime.

Individual children differ in their need for sleep. There may be as much as two or three hours difference in sleep requirements in children. Watch for the signs, advises Newton, which indicate that he is ready for bed. Fussing and irritability, whining, quarreling, bumping into things more than usual may be signs of fatigue.6

It is important that the child knows what is expected of him at bedtime (as well as at any other time). And it helps when he can count on some kind of a ritual. Choose whatever seems most pleasant and relaxing; a short walk, a bath, reading a story, a snack*

Diet itself may have an influence on a person's sleeping behavior. With all the prepared and refined foods on the shelves these days, it is easy for children to fill up on lesser foods rather than to receive a wholesome diet. The child may therefore be deficient in one or more essential nutrients. Irritability or excitability may also be caused by an allergic reaction to food or food additives. Numerous books on the subject of nutrition are now available at health food stores. A consultation with a doctor of natural or preventive medicine may be well worthwhile.

Experiments by psychologists show that we remember through our sleep the words spoken at bedtime. Newton, therefore, cautions never to make bedtime a punishment. This does not mean, of course, that discipline should not be used when necessary. But once the child has been sent to bed as a disciplinary measure, he may well associate it with unpleasantness, and naturally put up more of a resistance.6

The child may resist going to sleep if he has not had enough loving and attention from his parents. Bedtime can thus be a good opportunity to spend some truly relaxing moments with the child. Make him feel that for that little while he can have full possession of his parents' time. Doing this at short sessions during the day may also help considerably.

A mother wrote me of the following experiences she has had with bedtime rituals with her children.

When my four-year-old daughter (she is fifteen now) napped, it was often in our bed. I would lie down with her and usually read a story. One afternoon as we were getting ready to nap she asked, "Can we have a little talk first?" Somehow I never

---

*The advice of having a calm time prior to bedtime is generally accepted as wise. In a pediatric textbook of the 1850's, however, the advice was given that children should run around for half an hour before bedtime. This would then insure a good night's sleep.

forgot this and have often thought that just as conversation and relaxation are an enjoyable part of sharing the bed for parents, so it must also be for children. When I think of it we always precede our sleep, nighttime or naptime, with a little talk, whether the children are sleeping with us or in their own beds.

Lately our present four year old has been talking a lot before going to sleep. He talks primarily with his Daddy. This serves a good purpose because Daddy doesn't get a chance to hear him well until the rest of the noisy brothers and sisters are out of the way. The child's stories amuse my husband and it relaxes him so his mood is more restful for the remainder of the evening. Maybe a lot of other Daddies could unwind in this way and respond to the needs of their children at the same time.

I just asked my fifteen-year-old daughter if she remembered the incident I referred to in the first paragraph. She said, "Yes," although she may have cheated a bit by reading her baby book because it is among the cherished things I've recorded. Maintaining good relations with a teenage daughter isn't easy. I'm grateful for whatever communication we established during her first five years of life, even when it involved giving up my sleep, marital privacy, and all the heated discussions on childrearing with my contemporaries in which I was always the underdog. I'm still the minority report at the bridge games and coffee parties. But the role isn't uncomfortable because we've experienced a measure of success while putting our ideas to work.

For several months when our older daughter was five years old, she asked both my husband and me to lie by her, one on each side, till she fell asleep. She would put an arm on each of us, give us a hug, and say, "I'm going to sleep with my Mama and Papa right next to me. Goodnight!"

When my husband is not at home, I'll lie next to her and often she asks, "Tell me about when you were a little girl." Or sometimes we discuss a particular incident, happy, sad, or distressing, that happened during the day.

I also find it interesting to observe that when I am putting our younger girl to bed, if my husband is not at home, Yvonne, our older child, will take her books, or dolls, or toys and sit on the bed, too, until I get up after Michelle has gone to sleep.

115

Bedtime can be smooth. It might take several years and several children to learn this fact, but it is possible, as several mothers of large families have attested. And so when you falter while you are trying, take a deep breath and try again. It is worth it.

BEDTIME WITH MICHAEL by Carole Sheron

The following letter was taken from the *La Leche League News* of May, 1974. Mothers may smile as I did when I read it. Aside from it's being quite humorous, it rings such a true bell with respect to the questions and answers and emotions at bedtime with a little child.

I had saved putting him to bed until last because he is the hardest. Michael Patrick. . .three years old. His daddy and I call him the blond bombshell. His five brothers and sisters have all been individually Bible-lessoned, storied, prayered, watered, and tucked in. Michael is sitting on his bed, impatiently waiting for me to lie down with him. I look over to where his adopted brother, four months younger, is already asleep; curled into a little brown ball. Raised in a foster home for twenty months, he has always gone to sleep like a model child. I'm tired from a busy day; all I want is a leisurely bath and to go to bed early. Michael is urging me to "hurry up and lie down with me" and I wonder where I went wrong. Why won't this child go to bed by himself?

Michael wants a song. But it's not that simple. He wants me to play my guitar and sing. Two choruses of "I've Been Working on the Railroad." Later, I carefully and logically explain that Mommy wants to take a bath and caution Michael that he is to stay in bed until Mommy finishes and then I'll lie down with him again. Blue eyes regard me solemnly and blond hair bobs as he nods his consent, but as I walk out the door he warns me, "A fast bath!"

The water is running into the tub and I'm pinning my hair up when I hear the familiar pitter-patter of hurried footsteps down the hall to my bedroom, a satisfied "thump" and I know he's in my bed. I take a hurried bath (is there any other kind?), dress, retrieve Michael from my bed, and we start all over again.

"I thought you promised Mommy to stay in your bed until I finished my bath?"

"I did, Mommy. But then when you were gone, I got a'scared and zoomed to your room."

Pretty soon we're both tucked into Michael's single bed. Very cozy. Nurtured on the closeness of the nursing relationship, Michael is a toucher. His arms are wrapped around my neck, his legs plopped across mine, his silky blond hair snuggled against my cheek. I savor the moment, but also wish he'd hurry and go to sleep. I have things to do and I'm tired.

The silence lasts but a minute. "Mommy. . .Your teeth look pretty and clean."

"Thank you, Michael. I just brushed them."

"Mommy. . .why does teeth get dirty?"

"Because food gets on them." Silence again. Then, "Mommy . . .how does water get off your toothbrush after you put it away in the cupboard?" Mentally I discard the word "evaporation" and answer, "Because the air moves around it inside the cupboard and dries it off." Silence again.

"Mommy. . .how did God make the first man?" I explain the story of creation, how the first man was formed from the dust of the earth, how God breathed life into him and he became a living creature. Impish giggles! "Was his name Raymond Sheron?" (Daddy's name) "No, Michael, you know better than that. His name was Adam."

"I know the lady's name. Her name was Even." I suppress a chuckle. "Well, almost. Her name was Eve. She was a beautiful lady."

"Mommy. . .how was I made?"

Oh, wow! I'm tired, half asleep and I've got the story of reproduction ahead of me. Patiently and filled with the wonder and miracle of it myself, I carefully explain how Michael grew safe and warm inside of me until he was big enough and ready to be born.

"How did I get out of you?" I explain that he was born through a special opening made especially for that purpose. Silence for a moment, then "Where is the opening?" I explain. More silence. I wonder what he's going to ask next.

"Mommy. . .why don't pigs have hair?" My mind boggles

at the sudden change in subject. "Well," I begin gamely, "if pigs had hair like you and me, when they wallowed in the mud, it would get all stuck in their hair and make them messy." Thankfully he's satisfied with my improvised answer.

"Why did Mrs. Centers cut up her pig?" Long ago he spent the day with a friend the day they butchered their hog. I explained that they needed it for food.

"We don't do that, do we? We get our food from the store." We are vegetarians so the idea of killing animals for food was new to him. He seemed a little disturbed by it.

He turns over and snuggles down into his covers. I think the magic moment has arrived, but not yet. "Mommy. . ." And I am entertained with a long and complicated adventure story plucked from the world of "pretend" involving himself and his imaginary horse Trigger. As he talks his eyes get rounder and rounder and his eyebrows disappear under his long, blond bangs as his face becomes more animated. Finally the story is over, he begins to yawn. He turns toward me again, takes my hand in both of his and is almost instantly asleep.

Suddenly I am caught up by those feelings of tenderness and overwhelming good will that a sleeping child bestows. There is something about sleep that transforms children into angels. Tangled lashes lie against cheeks still soft and round with a hint of babyhood still lingering. I gently kiss the soft mouth that in infancy searched eagerly for my breast and the milk that was his sole nourishment for the first six months. At almost two years that same mouth was known on many inopportune occasions to demand, "I want to nurse." Usually in church or the supermarket. And then one day to sit up from nursing and lament, "I don't like it." And he was weaned.

As I slip quietly from his bed, I am suddenly aware of the instinct of children to demand what they need. Busy with five other children and a full day, were it not for his terrible bedtime habits, I might not have found time for this special hour with Michael, for cuddling and just learning to know him. I thank God that he was born healthy, and bright, and whole, and even the knowledge that he'll probably be back in our bed before midnight can't destroy the peace that I feel at this moment.

FEAR OF THE DARK

Why are children afraid of the dark? Kenny and Schreiter's explanation makes it very clear:

Fear of the dark is very prevalent in childhood, from age two months to almost age eight. Darkness shrouds the normal visual and depth-perception cues that give the child his orientation within the environment. Not only do cues for the environment vanish, but even the child's own body vanishes, making him as invisible as the rest of the world. This situation produces anxiety. The child is left with only sounds and touch. But severing the visual from the auditory sense, sight from hearing, causes a great deal of anxiety. It seems that during light hours the child attends more to sight than to hearing; he understands sound stimuli only in reference to a seen object. Hence in the dark he has trouble connecting noises with their visual source. With the world of sight gone, the child is left with the world of sounds—the world of the wind, animal noises, and sirens—a world he could not attend to during the day. To make matters worse, the child is often "privileged" with his own room and confined in his own bed. This means no older person is there to reassure or protect him against the things that go "bump" in the night. But even the presence of another person in the room may not be enough. Usually children end up by scurrying into bed with the other person. Why? When darkness has taken sight, when sound is threatening, then touch is all that is left. It is a return to a period when things were not so threatening, when being curled up in the womb was a way of life. The child will move in with whoever is close—preferably the parents, although an older brother or sister will do.[7]

According to Bowlby, blind children are evidently more than usually afraid of such common fear-arousing situations as mechanical noises, thunder and wind. The principle reason, he feels, is that their contact with the world depends greatly on touch. When out of contact with their attachment figure, usually their mother, they may therefore experience more intense fright.[8]

The very young child does not have a past experience upon which to rely. To him if something is out of sight, it does not exist any more. Mothers know from experience that their very young children go through a stage of crying frantically when they leave the room momentarily. Even mother's voice, calling from another room, is not enough to calm her child. Most children go through this stage. Should the child awaken at night, he experiences these same fears of having lost his mother.

As the child grows older, he is less likely to be upset by separation. He becomes more able to understand that his mother will return. His nighttime fears are then not primarily based on fear of separation, as is true in the case of the younger child, but on fears aroused by his imagination, or other forms of anxiety. Indeed, fear of dark and of being alone is a feeling that most of us never quite master completely.9

FEAR IN FALLING ASLEEP

According to Luce and Segal, falling asleep is probably a more intense experience for children and adolescents than for mature people. The brain of a child is developing rapidly; it will triple in size from birth to age six. The nervous system is learning everything from bodily control to speech and other complicated skills, such as control over feelings. "With this internal ferment of growing," write Luce and Segal, "a child lies down to rest and he feels a variety of sensations. As a person drifts down into sleep, the brain is changing its functions. Certain brain cells seem to let go of their controls spasmodically. The result is a sudden convulsive jerk of the body. The half-asleep person may think he is falling, and wake up with a start. To a child, the sensation of falling may be both real and frightening. And this is just one of the sharp and unfamiliar sensations that come from the normal activity going on within the child's body and brain."10

Falling asleep may be especially frightening to the child who is alone in his room. He may resist going to bed because he vaguely remembers this fear, yet he is unable to explain it to an adult. It would be ridiculous to tell him "there is nothing to be afraid of," if he is experiencing fright. Fear is a real feeling, and should not be lightly dismissed, or ridiculed. Have we not ourselves at one time or another felt resentful, hurt, lonely when someone did not take our fear seriously?

Fear at bedtime may be aroused by innocent remarks made by a parent. One mother used to say to her son, "Goodnight, and don't let the bedbugs bite." To the utter perplexity of his parents this boy used to wake up screaming that there were bugs in his bedroom. His father would then go in the room and "kill" all the bugs. After that the boy went off to sleep again. Nonetheless it was a most disturbing experience for everyone. His behavior remained a mystery until a friend overheard the boy's mother repeat her goodnight diction.

Some children may learn to fear sleep or have fears while going to sleep because of the possibility of death expressed in some bedtime prayers.[11]

> Now I lay me down to sleep
> I pray the Lord my soul to keep.
> If I should die before I wake,
> I pray the Lord my soul to take.

The bedtime fears with which some adults are plagued and for which they perform magical rituals, may well have their origin in bed and nighttime fears experienced in childhood. Some of these rituals include locking all the windows, keeping a certain light on, drinking some warm milk, placing clothing in a certain order, closing all the closet doors, etc. These are rituals which, when broken, leave a feeling of uncertainty or threat within the person; they are performed so that nightly protection is obtained.

I believe that when children are allowed to fall asleep in the presence of another person, preferably a loving adult, the possibility of fear in falling asleep will be minimized, and will most likely be nonexistent.

WHEN FATHER IS AWAY

Some books on childrearing make it a point to warn mother against allowing children to sleep with her, even when Dad is away on a trip, lest the children will come to look forward to seeing Daddy off. If it is the only time that the children get to enter the family bed, the advice might indeed be justified. But when I mentioned this to mothers whose children sleep off and on in the family bed, all were taken aback and exclaimed, "But this is not true. Nothing will take the place of Daddy!"

THE OLDER CHILD JOINS THE FAMILY BED

Some parents who have reared their child or children the recommended way, "owned cribs and let him scream it out," and then have realized the more understanding approach, have tried to recap-

121

ture the stages of development which they feel were insufficiently fulfilled.

When parents thus decide to start having their youngster sleep with them or with siblings, after the child is accustomed to sleeping by himself, they should remember that it is a new experience for the child as well as for them. The adults, however, know what is happening but the youngster doesn't. The child may associate his parents' or siblings' bed only with games and rough housing, and his own bed with security and sleep. It may take him several nights, perhaps even several weeks, until he becomes totally accustomed to sleeping with others.

I have found with my own child, Yvonne, who did not join us until she was almost two and a half years old, that it was an endless struggle to ask her to lie still and be quiet. So I finally decided to let her wiggle and talk, within reason, and I found that after a while she would fall asleep anyway. Her sleep came no later than if I had asked her repeatedly to remain quiet and still. And we have had no nagging or tension. As she became older, she quieted down considerably. She is six now. At bedtime we will read a story, talk a bit, and then I ask her to lie on her side and talk no more. My husband or I will still usually stay with her until she has fallen asleep.

GUESTS FOR DINNER

What do you do when you have dinner guests, and your youngsters, who have to go to bed, are used to having you with them while they fall asleep? We only have dinner or after-dinner guests when my husband is home. Then when the children are ready for sleep, I make sure that there is enough to drink and eat for the adults, and I quietly disappear. As soon as the youngsters are asleep I re-appear. And in parenthesis I add that after the hustle and bustle of trying to get the house cleaned up, cooking dinner, setting the table—in the meantime keeping children away from the stove, the waste paper basket, and the table, plus getting them ready for bed—it is quite refreshing to lie down with them for a little while. Guests and friends are important and fun to have. (It's also exciting for the children. All the more reason not to send them away from the party to go to sleep by themselves.) But the ultimate happiness of one's children should come first. With a little forethought and explanation things can usually be worked out to the satisfaction of all concerned. I usually wait just a little bit past the children's regular bedtime before putting them to bed, so that I may be gone no more than a short while.

THE CHILD TOO OLD TO JOIN THE FAMILY BED

After a certain age, some children may not want to actually join the family bed. A loving little talk and attention, and a friendly backrub at bedtime may be a good way to end the day for these children. Dr. Riordan, a La Leche League Medical Advisor, suggests that such a friendly backrub at bedtime is often the most effective and least expensive psychological therapy when things haven't gone smoothly between parent and child that day. (*LLL News*, Sept. '70)

He further says that by rubbing the child's back, the parent shows he still cares for the youngster, and the child is reassured that he's not an undesirable thing—nobody touches an undesirable thing.

A backrub is relaxing. It gives time for a little conversing between parent and child, which they may not have had during the daytime hours when there are so many interruptions.

THE BABY WHO REFUSES PARENTS' BED

Occasionally we hear of the older baby who is used to sleeping in his own crib and simply refuses to sleep in his parents' bed. He wiggles and struggles and cries and screams. No sooner has he been put in his crib than he quiets down and goes to sleep, perhaps with a favorite toy or blanket. The parents feel rejected and resentful toward the baby that he should prefer his crib and blanket to them. They may feel that he is disowning them.

While this entire book attempts to explain why parents should not struggle to keep children *out* of the parental bed, it is ironic that we should have to discuss the case of parents who struggle to keep him *in* the family bed.

I have no simple solution with respect to this situation, mainly because I feel there are factors involved which we do not know, but which make a baby act in this manner. The most important thing to remember is that love does persevere and conquer all. His crib and blanket he will outgrow, but his parents' love he will always have. Perhaps the child will be content to sleep with his parents if he is allowed to keep his blanket with him; or perhaps the crib can be taken down, and baby can sleep on a mattress in a corner of his or their room. The parent can lie next to the child to give him a sense of human closeness while he falls asleep.

It will be wise to realize also that little babies are individuals with individual wants and needs which must be respected. Yes, we must guide them along the best routes. But sometimes, for unknown reasons, the child does not respond directly. All we can do then is to be patient and above all else, love.

WHEN A PARENT OR CHILD IS ILL

A parent of a child who is ill, unless very ill, will benefit greatly from having the family accustomed to sleeping together. Many a wakeful night of floor-walking has been averted because a feverish, unhappy child has been able to snuggle up to his parents and if he were still breastfeeding, nurse himself off to sleep. More so than when he is well, a child who does *not* feel well seeks and needs the presence of his mother. And many mothers have expressed the good feeling of being right at hand when a child has become ill at night. It has also given parents a sense of comfort to know that they were aware at all times of the child's well being. A mother writes, "Our middle child has bronchial complications with about every cold. We all feel better having her sleep with us during the nights when breathing is a chore for her. I'm able to keep her propped up on a pillow between us, and she sleeps better knowing that we're next to her."

For the Mom who does not feel well herself it means being able to remain in bed, usually without even having to sit up, should one of the children or the baby need attention. When one is tired or ill, that horizontal position is heavenly and most appreciated, and the thought of possibly having to get up, most unwelcome.

CONCLUSION

Many cultures differ in their childrearing customs and practices. The age at which a child no longer sleeps next to his mother also differs greatly among various societies. I do not recall reading anywhere, however, of older children sleeping isolated from one another, except in our Western world or among those peoples greatly influenced by our culture.

Our society tends to ignore a child's need for the presence of another person at night. Enforced loneliness is greatly encouraged even when he is not ready to be separated. Many children, through nature's wise efforts, make attempts to counter this unnatural situation. But the taboo against co-family sleeping is so strong, that every effort is made to find material substitutes with which the child is supposed to be content, happy and satisfied. But what could ever truly take the place of a real person, one whose love is transmitted by spirit and by touch? For the best for the child, there is no substitute.

SIBLINGS

Sometimes I do, sometimes I don't," says four-year-old Vivette, as she tells her mother that this night she wants to sleep with her older sister, instead of in her parents' bed. And this is how weaning from the parental bed begins, gradually, at the child's own pace. It can be so gradual that some parents have a hard time remembering just when it happened.

The age at which this takes place depends entirely on the individual child. It also depends on whether he has another sibling with whom to sleep, and whether he has slept in his parents' bed from birth on.

It seems that after a certain age, the emotionally stable child no longer needs the direct, touching security of his parents, but will be content to sleep away from them as long as he can sleep with some other person.

Parents have found that those children who had their own bed from birth on, but were allowed to visit the parental bed occasionally tend to keep returning to the family bed much longer than those children who slept with their parents from birth on. The fear, wrote several parents, that sleeping with the parents would become an unbreakable habit, was not substantiated in our case.

Parents have also noticed that whenever an older child has had a problem he will return to sleep with them for a while until the problem solves itself. Then he is back to his own room again.

127

It is a very common reaction for a human being who finds himself in a situation with which he cannot cope, to regress to an older, familiar form of behavior.[1]

Many parents feel that the body contact of siblings sleeping together makes for a more peaceful home. "Among other things," wrote a parent, "we've found that when two children sleep together they get along better the next day. We feel it's fostering a closer relationship between them, and nightmares and other nighttime disturbances are really rare."

Another mother said, "I have two children who fought a great deal and did not like to sleep with anyone. Due to necessity, these two children at ages five and six had to start sharing the same bed. They began to get along much better. They didn't even mind snuggling with each other after a while. I later found out that my brother had this same experience with his two daughters. At ages six and seven, they needed to sleep together to make room for another baby. He remarked how much better the two girls had gotten along since they began to sleep together."

Dr. Spock feels that the main disadvantage of two young children sleeping in the same room is that they are apt to wake each other up at the wrong times.[2] Not one of the answers to the question "What are your experiences of having siblings sleep together?" however, mentioned this particular problem. As a matter of fact, most answered in the positive tone. "They all sleep in the same room, boys and girls. No problems."

A few mothers mentioned that their family plays musical beds. "My children sleep with whomever they feel like. It makes for a happy situation. They especially like to take turns sleeping with the baby (the youngest) of the family."

One mother who decided to put her two boys in one bedroom wrote, "Our boys sleep in the same room now, and they do fight. But they also seem much closer than we expected."

The question may be raised, is sibling rivalry normal? To this Dr. Lee Salk answers that since in our Western world it is common, it is statistically normal. He feels that it is a struggle for recognition and attention from any adult caring for them.[3] Our society has not made it easy for children. Usually no grandparents, aunts, nor uncles live with or close to the young family. These relatives cannot share in the love and attention given to the young ones on a daily basis. I have repeatedly read in the studies of anthropologists that in groups in which the extended family lives with or near the nuclear family, in which not one but many adults take responsibility for the children, sibling rivalry exists very little or not at all.

Another parent whose children now sleep together commented, "Sleeping together definitely improved the relationship. Now they *want* to sleep together."

Another mother wrote about her three-year-old son: "When Claude was three he asked for his own bed in his brother's room. He had a choice of either sharing a bed with his brother or getting a bed of his own. He tried both, and settled for sleeping with his nine-year-old brother."

Some nursing children are perfectly happy to sleep with older siblings when Mom is not around to nurse them off to sleep. "When my husband and I are out for the evening," wrote a breastfeeding mother, "my thirteen-month-old baby is content to go to sleep with one of his brothers or his sister."

One parent volunteered to give several reasons on the question of siblings sleeping together. "All positive," she remarked. "I have no real negative reactions."

1. Nobody is afraid at night from noises, thunder, lightning, or of being alone in a dark room.
2. Body warmth of one another helps them to sleep soundly, especially the smaller children who come uncovered so easily.
3. They are learning to share sleeping quarters, which is something they will have to do later on when they go camping, and then when they get married. Not one of my children has ever demanded "his own bed," or "his own room." This could be due also to the fact that my husband and I share the family bed, and the children think this is the only way to sleep.
4. The youngest child feels cared for and the older ones learn to take care of the needs of their siblings, such as bringing a glass of water—many of the things that mother would have to do during the course of the evening or the night.

This mother has six children ranging from one year to eighteen years.

A beautiful mother of nine children told me that after everyone is bedded down, they pray the day's final prayer together before drifting off to sleep. It ends the day peacefully.

Sleeping together calls for sharing, and consideration of others. When children have a chance to learn this within the family unit, it will strengthen them as individuals, as members of the family, and the family as a whole will be stronger.

Upon graduation from the family bed at a time when he no longer needs the particular presence of his parents, a child will frequently choose to sleep with and find comfort in being with his brothers and sisters.

One mother suggested that a pet such as a dog or cat may make a sibling substitute for the only child who has outgrown the family bed.

Our present day society is aiming for educating and rearing the child as a strong, independent individual. He has his own activities, his own playthings, his own schedules, sometimes his own mealtimes. He is part of and yet alone in his position in his family. Sleeping together will therefore be the logical conclusion of the day and of importance in keeping each child in touch with the other members of the family.

Much can be said for the children of a family who enjoy each other's presence and find comfort in it.

MARITAL RELATIONS

Kindness in words creates confidence.
Kindness in thinking creates profoundness.
Kindness in giving creates love.

It comes as no surprise that one of the first questions concerning children in the parental bed is, "But what about one's sex life?"

Our country is sex-oriented. The breasts are associated with sex instead of a source of life for a newborn infant. The bed is frequently associated with "going to bed with someone" or "having sex with someone." We read in popular magazines how the plump woman enjoys sex more than the skinny woman. We can gauge our sex life with charts in articles which go into detail showing how many times a week or month sex is "normal." Article after article is printed in popular publications on the subject of sex. It is even believed by countless people, write Luce and Segal, that sex is essential to a good night's sleep.

The fact that children sleep with their parents is considered by many people to be highly indecent and immoral. Yet, in spite of today's frowning on children in the parental bed or in their siblings' beds, at a time when separate beds and bedrooms are a must supposedly to "guard" children and give them a moral upbringing, sexual promiscuity among teenagers and adults knows almost no limits, even though premarital or extra-marital sexual relations are greatly taboo.

This strong interest in sex may, in part, be the direct result of the minimal physical contact which so many of the younger generation have received during infancy. Perhaps an inner drive is attempting to repair the damage of too little bodily stimulation during childhood.

In a cross-cultural study on childrearing practices, compiled by James W. Presscott, Ph.D., it was pointed out that there seems to be a direct correlation between the amount of body pleasure during infancy, the practice of premarital sexual behavior, and adult interpersonal relations. In most of the societies which were studied, the following pattern was observed: minimal holding, caressing, and fondling of infants would in most cases result in violent adult interpersonal behavior patterns, unless premarital sexual relations were socially accepted and tolerated. Conversely, those societies which gave a great deal of physical attention to the infant were characterized by minimal adult interpersonal violence.[1]

I have frequently observed in the anthropological reports which I have read, a correlation between the violence which a people exhibit in their everyday living, i.e. disharmony among members of a family or tribe, active warring, torturing of the enemy, violent or painful initiation rites, and their interest in sex. Namely, their sexual drives seemed to be stronger in many instances than was the case among people who were peaceful, lived harmoniously, and whose total image revealed gentleness. Dr. Prescott concludes his report by saying that he feels interpersonal violence in human societies can be minimized by maximizing physical affection, i.e. body pleasure, during infancy and adolescence.[2] Likewise, Janov expresses the opinion that a loved child does not grow up into an adult with an insatiable craving for sex. The child, says Janov, has been held and caressed by his parents and does not need to use sex to satisfy that early need.[3]

Adults' possessive interest in sex and the inability to tolerate interferences—one of these being children in the parental bed—which are so predominant in our society may thus be a manifestation of unfulfilled sensory stimulation during their infancy.

One mother wrote, "I feel that by keeping children a little bit longer in the parental bed, perhaps they will stay a bit longer out of a premarital bed. Maybe some of those adolescent kids who crawl into bed with each other are really looking for Mama, except Mama was never there." Perhaps this mother instinctively felt there is a connection between the teenage search for physical contact and a lack of sufficient infant physical contact, which could be the result of separate sleeping, bottlefeeding, schedules, and numerous mother-substitute gadgets.

CROSS-CULTURAL OBSERVATION

The taboos that society places upon sexual matters are not the result of biological heredity, rather they are the result of cultural training.[4] Although in our society it is strongly believed that when children observe sexual relations such observations may lead to neuroses later in the child's life, other societies hold quite different views. Newton adds that if the observing of the primal act is really as upsetting as some psychoanalysts maintain, large numbers of historical and traditional peoples would have been neurotic.[5]

There are, indeed, cultures other than the Western society in which great pains are taken to avoid children's observation and indulgence in sex. However, from what I have deduced through my reading, adult neurosis has not been mentioned as the reason for the avoidance.

On the other hand, there are societies in which sex is an encouraged subject. Children are allowed to observe sexual behavior and to participate in the discussion of sexual matters. The older children of the Chewaos in Africa build little huts some distance from the village, and there with complete approval of the parents, play at being husband and wife. It is believed by this tribe that unless children begin to exercise themselves sexually early in life, they will never have children.[6] Between the two extremes there are many variances with respect to permitting observation of adult sex, and indulgence in child sex, and self-stimulation. All members of the Pukapukan household sleep in the same room under one mosquito net, and although some parents wait until they think the children are asleep, there are frequent opportunities for youngsters to observe sexual activities.[7]

In most societies, however, couples seek some sort of seclusion for sexual intercourse.[8] This no doubt serves in many instances as assurance against interruptions.

As a result of such great differences in sexual training, adult members of different societies have quite varied opinions as to what is proper or normal or immoral or unnatural in sexual relations.[9] An adult may be quite shocked or perplexed at the attitudes and customs of another people. This shows clearly in a letter by a mother of Rhodesia in which she expresses feelings of disbelief at the Western taboo of co-family sleeping. "Our quarters here consist of one room, and naturally we all sleep in it." She further explains that their child is very much aware of adult sex, but that neither she nor her husband had ever thought that it would be harmful to him. "My husband and I were brought up in the same fashion. It hasn't given my husband a complex about sex." She ends her perplexed letter by asking the American doctor to whom this letter was directed, "And what is an Oedipus complex?"[10]

It is certainly not my intention to advocate parental sexual relations in the presence of one's children or any children. However, I have included this brief cross-cultural sample of the primal act to illustrate that just because our society feels it is immoral or psyche damaging—as children in the parental bed is thought to be—it may not in fact be so. The presentation of these examples shows that, in fact, other peoples do just that which our culture discourages and yet seem to produce quite stable members for their societies.

HISTORICAL OBSERVATION

Our next questions then is why and when did the strong taboo of these sexual matters develop.*

Evidence indicates, according to Ryerson, that childrearing methods prior to 1750 with respect to the permissiveness of oral, anal, sexual and dependence training, closely approached the permissiveness of primitive societies.[11] In other words, a child was breastfed for at least a year and a half, and slept with another person, usually his mother. Toilet training was not hastened. Self-stimulation and observation of sex was not forbidden, and independence was not forced prematurely.

This picture totally changes between 1750 and 1900. In the mid-eighteenth century the patriarchal family, which included father, mother, children, grandparents, aunts, servants began to be replaced by the nuclear family. "In this small, intimate environment," says Ryerson, "the child competed more directly with the parent of the same sex for the attention of the other parent. With the greater intimacy between parents and children in the nuclear family, underlying fear of incest increased. Therefore the child's sexual

---

*It is important that the reader shall read the chapter on the "History of Childhood and Family Sleeping Customs," since it will familiarize him more completely with the total historical picture.

expressions were dealt with more strictly."[12]

During this period there was a great decrease in the once so relaxed transition phase. Breastfeeding was curtailed, toilet training was hastened. The observation of the sex act and the practice of self-stimulation became taboo. Much negative attention was given to the bodily functions and needs in the form of restriction or in the fact that they were ignored. Separate sleeping from a very young age became more and more "the thing" to do, especially among the upper and upper middle class families. Children in this situation did not "grow up" being familiar with adult sex. They therefore were not likely to observe sexual intercourse. Should such a child then, without education or previous association, see his parents during sexual intercourse, he might have no other reference than associating the sex act with violent interpersonal relations.

Around 1900 Sigmund Freud presented his theory on psychopathology. He saw the observation of the primal scene as an important contributing factor to neuroses. However, the role of observation of sexual intercourse in neuroses may not be its observation per se, but rather the fact that the child did not observe this from birth on.* Also, the drastic reduction in the transition phase and gratification of the infant's emotional needs and physical needs may be important contributing factors in psychopathology.[13]

"This," writes Bowlby, "Freud began to realize toward the end of his professional life. However, by that time a substantial body of psychoanalytic theory was already being taught, and Freud's ideas on separation anxiety [thus also separate sleeping, forced independence, etc.] came too late to influence the development of the schools of thought based on his previous theory of which anxiety, castration anxiety, and superego anxiety, were the corner stones."[14]

By 1940, reports of clinical observations were published which drew attention to the pathogenic significance of separation experiences. Nevertheless, these observations have been extremely slow to gain a central place in psychoanalytic theorizing.[15]

---

*Certainly, Ford and Beach have cited a number of ethnic groups in which marital sexual relations are not hidden from the children.

135

PRIVATE CONVERSATIONS

The belief is held by many that parents should have their own private bedroom for sexual relationships and private, quiet talk as a necessity for a sound, happy marriage. In our society, most couples "enjoy" a considerable amount of bedroom privacy since most children sleep away from the master bedroom. Yet in 1960 the divorce rate was twenty-six divorces for every one hundred marriages. And a mere fifteen years later, 1975, a new record had been set: forty-eight divorces for every one hundred marriages.[16]

To parents who agree to co-family sleeping, there seems to be no particular problem if they want to talk for a while before they go to sleep. If the conversation revolves around a subject that the children should not hear, they discuss it before going to bed. Otherwise, parents remarked, the children frequently sleep through their conversing.

If the youngsters should awaken, they simply listen, or join the conversation, and fall asleep again when mother and father close their eyes for the night. When a child sleeps with his parents, I believe there need not be the fear of "suppose he wakes up, we'll never get him back to sleep!" Many children all too eagerly love to snuggle up in the dark of the night, and fall asleep against another person.

MARITAL RELATIONS

We have to accept the fact that in our society the observation by children of their parents' sexual activities is not accepted; our style of living, morals and taboos are not designed to compensate for this. Psychiatrists therefore strongly urge parents not to have relations while the children are in their bed or room, even when the child seems to be asleep. It is for this reason that most parents choose to make love in a place where the children past infancy are not present.

The exchange of marital relations does not necessarily have to take place in the master bed. Parents who enjoy sleeping with their children have found it to be of no difficulty at all to make other arrangements for sexual relations, and a surprising number indicated that maturity, good humor or patience play an important part in their adaptability.

One mother emphasized the non-urgency of it all. If the child awakens or just plainly doesn't want to go to sleep, the sexual relations will have to be forgotten for that day. She comments, "There is always tomorrow, next week. Don't blame postponement on the child." She further emphasized that since they have two teenagers, she and her husband have found there to be many indications for foregoing immediate expression of sexual love. Sometimes one of the children wants to stay up and talk, or wanders around the house late at night. "It helps if you're not obsessed with the idea that sexual relations MUST take place. If you're going to be married for a lifetime, sooner or later you'll get around to whatever has to be postponed right now."

Some parents feel that using the living room or cozy den, with wine and soft music, adds pleasant variety. Others move to a spare bed in the house, or move the child or children who were in their bed momentarily in with other siblings. With their extraordinary depth of sleep in the first half of the night, sleeping children are often unaware even of being transported by their parents.[17]

Some families have the children begin the night away from the parental bed. This gives the parents a few hours of privacy. A mother of a large family commented, "With seven children intimate moments require planning and sometimes plotting." And one father answered, "If the interest is great enough, a way can be found."

Another young father replied, "I used to think it was my privilege as a husband to sleep with my wife in one bed, by ourselves. However, I now realize that when a man begets children, he no longer is merely a husband, he is now also a father with responsibilities of a father. And my wife is no longer merely a wife, she is now a mother, with responsibilities of a mother. We have responsibilities now in which personal wants will at times have to be foregone."

And a thoughtful mother answered the question , "Do you feel that having children sleep in the parental bed interferes with your sexual relationship?" by saying, "Sometimes it interferes if you are referring to direct sexual intercourse. If sexual relationship refers to the total love relationship of sexually mature adults, then, no, since rearing our children is a primary aspect of our love and our relationship. Of course, expression of this love, though preferably physical, at times does have to suffice with verbal contact."

NATURAL FAMILY PLANNING

It is not only the presence of children, whether in the parental bed, or around the house, which could result in the foregoing of impulsive sexual relations. Many parents choose not to subject themselves to the known and unknown physical danger or moral responsibilities of artificial contraception. When they wish to limit the size of their family or postpone pregnancy, they use the highly effective method of natural family planning. This method is based on the bodily changes that take place within the woman, which indicate the fertile and infertile stages during the menstrual cycle. Natural family planning requires abstention of sexual intercourse during certain days of a woman's menstrual cycle. When used correctly, this method can be, according to Kippley, more effective than the use of condoms or a diaphragm, and as effective as the Pill. It is considered to be more effective than the mini-Pill and the IUD which are not as effective as the older and larger dosage pills. It has now been established that both the Pill and the IUD are abortifacts.

Those breastfeeding mothers who wish to benefit from the natural infertility through breastfeeding, are strongly advised to take their babies to bed with them. The child will suck frequently during the night, and further secure the suppression of ovulation. This is part of the "total mothering" picture which Sheila Kippley has described so warmly in her book *Breastfeeding and Natural Child Spacing: The Ecology of Natural Mothering*.

Many couples have found a new depth and meaning in their marriage when they have begun to practice natural family planning. Several years ago one such couple wished to share with others the meaning and knowledge they had obtained in their search for an effective natural method. Thus Sheila and John Kippley founded the Couple to Couple League (P.O. Box 11084, Cincinnati, Ohio 45211). Their manual, *The Art of Natural Family Planning*, has proven to be the answer to a search for an increasing number of couples.

Abstention from sexual intercourse, whether because of a nursing baby, a child in need, or a reason to prevent pregnancy, has meant for many a chance to mature and grow in love for each other and other members of the family.

INTERRUPTUS*

Parents of a very young breastfeeding infant may have noticed a mysterious occurrence when they are involved in sexual relations. In an article in *Psychology Today*, Dr. Krebs tells of the following experience which he encountered with both of his breastfed children. As soon as he and his wife began to make love, the newborn would wake up, begin to whimper, and soon break into a full cry. The baby's awakening seemed to be unrelated to any other cause such as hunger, noise or movement. At three months the mother conceived again. Baby was put on a bottle and quit waking up when the parents were having sexual relations.[18]

In response to this article I read the following letter:

Richard Krebs, M.D. has made some fascinating observations on infants awakening during parental sexual activity. I have been curious about this phenomenon from two points of view; first as a mother of two breastfed children, and second as an independent student of genetically predetermined behavior patterns in human beings, particularly the mother-child relationships.

As a La Leche League counselor, in extensive contact with large numbers of nursing mothers, I agree that this phenomenon is quite common. Having read of Jane Gooddall's observations of chimpanzees, in which the young physically interfere with males' copulation attempts with the juveniles' mothers (to the extent of even knocking them off), I wondered if this was another of the inherited behavior patterns. Indeed, I would go so far as to speculate that perhaps *Homo sapiens'* apparent proclivity towards privacy and nighttime sexual encounters might have been a reaction towards this juvenile interference, responding to the simultaneous development of sexual behavior sustaining the continuous pair-bond (which the chimps do not have).

Incidentally, I would also go so far as to disagree with the hypothesis that it is the odor of the mother's milk which arouses the infant. The simple test of this would be to have the mothers express their milk, while near the sleeping infants. If others' experience is like my own, I would guess that the infants would not awaken. Yet the same infants would awaken if the mother engaged in sexual intercourse in a separate room. It is my temporary hypothesis that this awakening is based upon a psychic extra sensory phenomenon. I believe it is possible that the mother is in constant mental contact with the child, and that sexual behavior so distracts her that the connection is broken, and the infant awakens "seeking" its mother.

I would further guess that if the mother allowed the child to remain in the bed near her during her sexual activity the child would not awaken. This would support the theory that the awakening is related to being close to the mother, rather than to prevent conception. Indeed the fact that conception is greatly, if not almost totally prevented by continuous lactation would indicate that that mechanism was already accounted for. What natural selection has not been able to account for is the apparently unique mammalian pattern in humans to leave their totally helpless infants in separate sleeping areas from the mothers. I am guessing that the awakening is the infant's way of insuring that the mother doesn't forget about it or abandon it.[19]

Certainly a thought-provoking letter. This peculiar mother-child relationship might be another manifestation of that mysterious link mentioned earlier when a nursing mother wakes up in anticipation of her child's awakening. Or the strange occurrence which nursing mothers relate, that of having a let-down at the same time their babies start crying, which is nothing unusual except that they may be doing their shopping while their babies are at home.

A happy birth has a good chance to result in a happy, relaxed mother-child couple. A happy, relaxed mother and child relationship has a good chance to result in a happy, relaxed husband-wife couple, which in turn has a good chance to result in a happy family. And a happy family means respect for one another's feelings and acceptance of occasional interference with respect to personal wants. In a situation such as this the sexual relationship between man and wife becomes a part of the total marriage picture. Happy children will then make this a complete and beautiful picture.

---

*From the article "Interruptus" by Dr. R. Krebs. *Psychology Today,* Jan. 1970, p. 153.

THE ADOPTED CHILD

Speak for the child because he can't always speak for himself.

"In the case of our adopted child," says one mother, "we felt that extra cuddling and togetherness during the hours in bed was the best way to break through emotional barriers. This child is bottlefed. I also lie down to bottlefeed him and cuddle at least once a day."

This kind of thinking also applies to the foster child, many of whom, like the adopted child, may have been very much deprived of the intimacy with another person which is so necessary for optimum human development.

In her book *Relactation: A Guide to Breastfeeding the Adopted Baby*, Elizabeth Hormann encourages adoptive mothers to take their babies to bed with them. It will not only result in the benefit of frequent nursing, thus additional stimulation to the breast, resulting in an increase in milk production, but also serve as a simulation of the biological mother-child relationship. While frequent nursing does have a good effect on milk supply, it is this relationship which is the essence of nursing, she says.[1]

In private correspondence, Mrs. Hormann has made reference to the many mothers who have written to her. They wrote that they keep their adopted babies with them all night to give them the body contact they may have missed in foster homes and institutions.

With the foregoing information in this book, it is thus clear that above all, the foster or adopted child should be welcomed not only into his new home, but into the family or siblings' bed as well, so that he will truly feel part of that family, and of the whole family of man.

"You have touched me. I have grown." How especially applicable to these children.

TESTIMONY BY MRS. C

We were expecting our third child when we met Greg, a six-month-old bi-racial baby. Greg was the younger brother of Jenny, our first adopted child. Jenny was then two years old.

Greg was a beautiful black baby, with large brown eyes and a sweet passive nature. Since he was related to our Jenny, we applied to adopt him, also. After eight months of concern for this little fellow, we were told we could not adopt him. He was placed in a Permanent Foster Care home. Although this was to have been a lifetime placement, it lasted only a year. Greg was then placed in another home and this placement, too, lasted only a year. By this time he was considered to be emotionally disturbed, and after a brief period of hospitalization he was placed in a diagnostic foster home for evaluation. He was by then three years old. By the grace of God, the mother who ran the diagnostic home realized that this was the child we had wanted to adopt, and she called us.

We could hardly contain our excitement at being able to see him again. Yet, we were filled with sorrow when we saw the sad physical and emotional condition into which he had deteriorated. He had changed so much. But when I picked him up, my arms remembered him and I knew that deep within him he was still that sweet baby. We immediately re-established contact with the welfare department and requested again to adopt him.

We were turned down many times. One reason, claimed the welfare department, was that we already had four children, and a child with this many emotional problems would need special attention. But we felt that having four children who would give him just that much more love and attention was an asset, not a liability.

Finally after many months of prayerful perseverance, Greg was placed in our home for adoption.

What a joy we knew as we brought him into the loving circle of brothers and sisters who had awaited the arrival of their new brother for so long!

By this time Greg was nearly four years old. Among his problems were the inability to keep food down, and to sleep through the night. It was also difficult for him to accept the normal, loving, touching that goes on in a close family. He had always been expected to sleep by himself in his own room. In our family we have no such "luxury," and quite soon, as he slept with one of his siblings, the insomnia problems disappeared. We also gave him backrubs. But while his sleep and eating problems improved, he regressed in many other accomplishments.

His independence rapidly deteriorated. He no longer could dress himself. He began to speak in baby talk. But we followed through and tried to fulfill each need as it arose.

Greg is now a healthy, cheerful, active eight year old. He enjoys a lot of physical contact, and doesn't think that a room of his own would be a privilege. That is just as well because with seven children, doubling up is something that we take for granted.

It is a pleasure to see how easy it is now for Greg to give love, how natural it is for him to put his arm around his little three-year-old brother Joey, and gently guide him, or sit him on his lap and read him a story. It is also just as natural for him to wrestle and play football with his thirteen-year-old brother Jeff. It means so much to us to observe the true inner independence which has developed in our Greg.

A large family necessitates closeness and that has been a blessing to all of us because it has encouraged us to re-evaluate our priorities and to relate to each other in terms of meeting emotional needs. Many of these needs are met through the concerned touch of someone who cares.

My husband's and my own background are middle class Swedish and English. This type of close relationship was not predominant in our cultural heritage. Experiencing this relationship, therefore, has been a lesson which we have been learning as we go along.

It has taken us fifteen years of childrearing to come to this point. Our first child, Tammy, came into our bed in the morning after she awakened. Our second child, Jeff, came into our bed during the night when he was old enough to crawl out of his crib. And so it went. Our three year old has slept with us every night since birth, although now he is spending an occasional night with an older brother or sister.

We wish now that we had been this casual and relaxed right from the beginning. We were silly enough at one time to think that we had to move from a two-bedroom home to a three-bedroom home when we had both a baby boy and a two-year-old girl. Afterwards we found to our chagrin that they did not like being in separate rooms and for a period of years we had a "spare" room, the room without which we thought we just could not do.

As we have grown and changed, we like to think that our changed values have had an impact on our older children, too. Perhaps we will not know to what extent this has taken place until they have children of their own. At the very least it has given them an alternative approach to childrearing, rather than just accepting society's current values. This lesson alone is part of the most precious heritage we can give to our children.

STEPPARENT

One mother, married for the second time, wrote: "My children's stepfather was uneasy the first couple of times sleeping with my children, though he had readily slept with his own. Now he is comfortable about it." No doubt the additional nocturnal closeness can also help to bring a new adult closer into the heart of the family.

HOSPITALIZATION OF A MEMBER
OF THE FAMILY

If you see someone without a smile, give him one of yours.

THE CHILD

What if the young child, who is accustomed to sleeping with someone, has to go to the hospital? There must be no question that every effort should be made for someone of the family to stay with that child at all times. This also means sleeping by him in the same hospital room, or even in his bed. At no time must parents be made to feel less needed when their child is hospitalized, for they alone will be a sign of normalcy in a very abnormal situation.

The possibility of hospitalization should never be the reason for not allowing the child in the parental bed, or in his siblings' beds. It is too rare an occasion.

It is known that when under the stress of childbirth, many parturient women react only to the voice of their assisting husbands, especially when giving birth in that strange environment surrounded by strangers: the hospital situation. Might it not be possible that children, also, when under the stress of illness and the strange surroundings of a hospital, will respond better to medical orders when they have been repeated by the parent?

The biological connection between parent and his child, says Salk, enhances communication and makes the parent especially well geared to the job of caring for his own child.[1]

Aside from the great benefits to the child, it is of psychological benefit to the parents or parent himself to be able to be with and care for his child during the latter's illness. Wanting to "do something," if only to stroke his hand, is a very natural desire of a parent who is concerned about his child's illness. Separation would only lead to frustration and perhaps, on the part of the child, a feeling of worthlessness. In this light, hospital administrators need to re-evaluate very thoroughly the common practice of separating the sick individual from his family and restricting the much-needed loving atmosphere, which only a family member can truly give, to a few visiting hours.

A young child may not be able to express the dire need he has to be touched and cared for by a loving member of the family. But an adult can and we should learn from his experiences. The mother of a friend of mine had to undergo a very serious operation. After the surgery she was in intensive care for several days. The patient was in extremely critical condition, but her daughter convinced the physician to allow her to be with her mother. During those critical days my friend stayed with her mother for the greater part of the day, and although the patient was not responding to anything that was said to her, my friend continually touched her mother by lightly stroking her hand, her arm or her head. The mother recuperated, and after she was well again, she told her daughter that during those first few days after surgery, she was in such extreme pain, that she frequently wanted to give up living. The only thing that gave her courage and hope was the loving, gentle touch of her daughter's hand.

The physician was so impressed by this that he now encourages immediate family to be with and touch his patients when they are in the hospital.

The wonderful book *Young Children in Hospital* by Dr. James Robertson, gives a thoroughly documented description of the deep need of the pre-schooler for the presence of his mother, especially during the time of hospitalization. It points out repeatedly that the child who has the constant presence of one of his parents is a happy patient, and picks up when he returns home where he left off with little sign that he has been away.

No matter how kind the nurses and doctors are, he needs the familiar security of his mother, in whom he places all his trust. Should she leave him, he becomes grief-stricken, unable to understand why those whom he needs so very much let him down. He experiences a sense of loss and abandonment. There has been a serious failure within that environment of love and security which the family provided before he went into the stranger hospital environment. He may seem to have adjusted to his hospital situation, but to a careful observer he will appear frightened, lonesome, and in urgent need of his mother.

Parents whose child needs to be hospitalized are strongly urged to read this book before their child's admission, or to contact "Children in Hospital," 31 Wilshire Park, Needham, MA 02192.

MOTHER

Hospitalization of the mother is usually extremely upsetting as far as the emotional welfare of the child, or children, is concerned. However, enlightened hospital administrators and personnel are beginning to recognize the importance of continued family inter-relationship. Children are permitted to visit their mothers, and fathers have unrestricted visiting privileges.

I personally know three mothers who were permitted to have their breastfeeding babies (one was three weeks old, one seven months old, and one twelve months old) as soon after surgery as they were capable of nursing.

With full cooperation of the nursing staff and doctors, each was permitted to have her baby in bed with her, also during the night. All three mothers were accustomed to sleeping with their children. The hospital personnel made special comments on how well the babies "behaved," and how quickly the mothers seemed to recuperate. In each case several friends of the mother in question helped out in the hospital room by taking care of the baby, i.e. changing him, playing with him, or taking him home for a few hours. "After all," remarked one understanding nurse, "nature does go on."

NIGHTTIME IS FOR SLEEPING!

Life is a perpetual instruction in cause and effect.
—Emerson

It is quiet. It is dark. It is night. Somewhere a young child awakens and speaks "Mama?" Mama stirs in her sleep. She reaches over and takes the child's hand. "Mama, I have to go to the bathroom."

"Fine, Sweetheart. Just slip quietly off the foot of the bed, and go to the bathroom. Mama will stay awake for you."

The youngster stands up. "But I want to go that way," pointing sideways to where other members of the family are sleeping.

"You will wake everyone up. Now please go quietly off the end of the bed."

"No! I want to go that way!"

Papa's dreams *are* interrupted. All are no longer asleep. All is not well.

Should a situation like this be tolerated? Of course not. Our role as parents does not stop at night and resume in the morning. There are times when children need guidance during the night as well as during the day. A situation like this should be no more tolerated than if the child were to be in his own room and start disturbing the quiet night, or start yelling in church, or throwing food at the dinner table, or refusing to comply with family rules.

A mother from Minnesota once said, "Think of how much animosity is directed at children who are ill-behaved. I don't want my children to have to bear this type of burden, so I teach them how to behave in our world."

Just because children are accepted and are welcome to sleep in the family bed, does not mean that they should be permitted to come and go as they please, when they please, and how they please, if their manner is disruptive of the smooth and peaceful functioning of the family. Of course we must at all times remember the emotional age of the child, his needs, and his capabilities. The child who wakes the family with his crying because he is in pain, or uncomfortable from a cold, should not be treated the same way as the child who decides to run in and out of his parents' bedroom or use the bed for a midnight trampoline spree, or willfully awakens the others with loud talking, balking or giggling.

The family that is not used to sleeping together may not be aware of the nighttime activities of young children. According to Luce and Segal, it is not unusual for a child of two or three years to stand up in bed, sit, talk, or even screech. This happens usually during a very deep sleep of the child, and he may be extremely hard to awaken. The child is thus not purposely disturbing the family. And the behavior is not abnormal. It is important for parents to realize this so that they will not reprimand a child who may be in the deepest sleep, and totally unaware of his doings.[1]

A six-month-old baby who is still awake for some midnight philosophizing should certainly not be treated the same way as the four year old who is gauging his parents. Nor should the ten year old be treated as a four year old. He may have some real emotional problems (real to *him*) which are keeping him awake, and about which he needs to talk right then and there. (At one a.m.? Yes, Mother!) As a matter of fact one parent told me that these midnight talks revealed the most and helped the best with their teenage youngster.

How then should one deal with a situation of this type? The child should be made to understand that the family sleeps at night. We all need our sleep, and it is not fair for one or more persons willfully or thoughtlessly to keep others awake. Daytime is for playing, laughing, talking, eating. Nighttime is for sleeping.

GUIDING THE CHILD

There are a great many books on the subject of childrearing and methods of discipline. Many of these books claim to have the best answer for rearing children. There are also those parents who have turned to the Holy Bible for guidance, and who feel it has given them the best answer for this difficult task.

Through my reading I have concluded, however, that it is not necessarily the method that is being used, but the security, consistency, love and respect which the parents exhibit to their children and others that will give the best results in rearing children. I believe that the strength lies in a feeling of security, of honesty of a parent within himself. To this basic sense of security the child will react. It is on this honesty that a strong relationship, one in which guidance could have the best chance of being successful, can be built.

We all strive toward a common goal; peace and harmony and health. There are many roads which lead toward this goal, and one may be no more right than the other. Whether one person or many persons follow that road, as long as it leads to the goal without violence, it is valid. But above all, each must not blindly succumb to another person's way, but must have faith in and use his own head and heart.

In our efforts to rear our children and do for them what is right, we do make mistakes. Childrearing involves one decision-making episode after another, and living with their outcomes. With no centuries old methods to guide us, it is no wonder that we make mistakes. Until a hundred years ago or so, childrearing customs were handed down from a mother to her children. A new mother could usually turn to her own mother for advice. Then, for better or for worse, childrearing customs began to change.

It is not surprising that parents are hesitant and wavering in their guiding actions and that they should experience a feeling of frustration or guilt if they do not live up to the ideal goal any of the childrearing methods set forth. The parent does not feel "Look at what I am doing to my *child*," but rather, "Look what *I* am doing to my child." And this, of course, is a tremendous responsibility and awareness of one's doings and capabilities.

I believe that much misbehavior of today's children is due to boredom, lack of playmates, and a seeking to fulfill a direct human relationship, love, which is not, for one reason or another, forthcoming. It might be helpful to ask, "Why is the child acting this way?" And one should seriously ask him too. Keep communications open and one may be surprised at the answers.

One proud mother told me of the following occurrence in her

151

family. After a particularly trying time, her husband sat down with their twelve-year-old son and asked him why he had been exhibiting such ill behavior. With careful questioning the boy's troubles were revealed. In conclusion it was the son who said to his father, "Dad, we are like a Walkie-Talkie. As long as we don't get too far away from one another and keep communications going, we'll be doing all right."

As we grow with our children, we mellow, we mature, and we see our children and our relationship with them in a more realistic nature. When our firstborn was two years old, she was *already* two. We said about our second born at that age that she was *only* two. We were realizing the physical, emotional and mental capabilities of the second child more realistically.

How, then, does one make a decision about which childrearing method to use? By reading, observing, discussing, and thinking. Remember the points you like (not because they satisfy you, but because they would be best for your child and your family situation) and set a goal.

I feel it is important for parents to realize not only their obligation to rear their children in a way which expresses security, consistency, love and respect, but also to realize the emotional and physical readiness of the child to receive the guidance.

CONCLUSION

The strongest principle of growth lies in human choice.
                                             —*George Eliot*

At the end of every winter, when tender new leaves appear on the trees and shrubs, when the robins return, and the daffodils bloom once more, we are surprised again that indeed time did not stand still after all; winter did pass. Winter is a time of intimacy, of cuddling, of feeling cozy near the fire in the fireplace. But as beautiful as winter is, it does at times seem long.

So, too, an infant will grow and slip out of your arms, will grow some more and slip out of your bed, will grow again and slip out of your home. Each phase will pass just as winter passes into spring, summer into autumn.

"We have grown together as parents to an understanding that our children need us at night," wrote a parent. "There have been times when the learning-growing process was difficult, sometimes for me, sometimes for my husband. It is often very beautiful, sometimes a little trying, but always worthwhile. The parental bed has become a FAMILY BED, which does not take away from the bed of love, but adds to it."

Should we be concerned about our neighbors' opinions if that which is involved is a solution for our family situation? The importance lies in finding arrangements which, with mature understanding of each other's and the children's needs, make everyone happy. The acceptance of this situation will lead to a relaxed happy atmosphere. "Happiness is the atmosphere in which all good affections grow." (Thomas Bray)

153

Ashley Montagu quoted James Plant as saying, "a conformity that is based on love will be free to develop into noncomformities, for the mentally healthy individual will not be bound to standards that conflict with his view of what is right."[1]

There is room in our society for experimentation which can enrich and strengthen family life. There is no reason to assume that our one culture has seized upon "an eternal sanity" and will stand in history as a solitary solution to the human problem.[2] Families are disregarding social customs. The family unit sleeps together and has found that doing so has enriched and strengthened the family life.

With the increasing popularity of the two-child or small family, I believe it to be especially important that the young child spend some time of the night in his parents' bed, and later sleep with his sibling or siblings, if not in the same bed, then in the same room. With our small families, and large houses with many rooms and bedrooms, it can be quite easy to become literally "out-of-touch" with one another.

Most of us can concur with the feeling of comfortable togetherness which somehow permeates the air when other loving people are present in the room. It is a pretty lonesome feeling to be by oneself, in a quiet room, surrounded by the darkness of night. The affluent have many rooms and many beds. The poor have few rooms and few beds. Who, however, is truly the wealthier? No amount of material things can truly soothe a lonely heart. Love and touch can.

Giving of ourselves should not be determined by a clock or schedule, but by human needs. In our society we are in danger of the tendency to separate ourselves from our children instead of allowing our children to separate themselves from us when they are ready. We should be the tree, strong and well-rooted, and they the seedlings which, when ready, will fall away with all potentialities of a new tree; strong and well-rooted.

There is much evidence to indicate the great importance of a long, fulfilled transition phase for the development of an emotionally stable person, one who will be inwardly strong. A baby's sleeping with its mother for the first few years of its life is an important aspect of the smooth functioning of the transition phase. Children who then initiate the separation will do so contentedly, whereas the child who is forced to leave before he is ready, may suffer from anxiety and the fear of losing his mother.[3]

Throughout a person's whole life, he has to have consideration, respect and a life in harmony with the world, be it spouse, family, friend, or environment. The preparation for this maturity begins the moment a child is born. Sleeping together is an active part of this educational process.

The need for privacy cannot be overlooked and parents have every right to it. However, it should not be placed above the needs of the children, nor satisfied in spite of the children, for they are our primary responsibility.

Although life seems easier for the modern family than for that of our great-great-grandparents, much, and acutally unfair, strain is placed on parents today. When the extended family lived together, a youngster in need of attention could always turn to another relative if his mother were not available. Children today have the same need for human attention; however, no matter how many children are in the family, there is usually only Mom and Dad around. Either parent should not have to be all-bearing, and yet there is no other choice. I believe we should seriously reconsider the great beneficial and wonderful position grandparents can fill. We need them as much as they need us, provided that the relationship is loving and harmonious.

Our children are constantly reminded that they should share. Even if they don't want to, we make them share, for not to share is socially frowned upon. Adults share too, says Montagu, until to do so becomes a burden or interferes with what they desire; then they rebel.[4]

Personal property need not be shared, but a child has every right to his share of the love and security of his parents when he needs it, be it during the day in the kitchen, or at night in bed.

And these precious years of sharing oneself with children are so short. With fewer pregnancies and longer life spans, most couples can now anticipate almost twenty years of "child-free" living.

At least 4,000 years ago an Egyptian scribe wrote of the disrespect, lack of control, and generally appalling behavior of the young people of that day. The gulf between the generations of today, however, has been matched few times in recorded history.[5] Perhaps a return to co-family sleeping would help to narrow this gap.

There is no such thing as rearing children in a "perfect" way. However, there are certain elements of childrearing which seem to lead more successfully to the growth of a happy, healthy person.

Natural childbirth, breastfeeding, co-family sleeping, good nutrition, love, and respect are some of these elements. Certainly children have been reared without some, or perhaps most of these. Fine children have been reared who did not sleep with their parents, who were bottlefed, whose mothers worked, but who received lots of love and respect from their parents. I am sure many parents will agree with me that with each additional child in the family we "improve" in our task of parenting. We need not feel threatened when others seem to have achieved a goal for which we are still striving. Nor need we feel resentful if others speak of their ways. But we should always seek for a goal and not be afraid to grow along with each child, for this will have benefit for the older children and ourselves.

It would be thoughtless to say simply, "Give your children that which they need," for deep within many of us lie needs which were not fulfilled during our own infancy, needs which, even as adults, we are still trying to fulfill—needs which are so strong that they surface when we are faced with our own children's demands, which make it difficult, if not impossible, for us to give our love freely to the child. It would be thoughtless because true maturing comes from within ourselves, not from without. We read frequently, "If you don't want to take the full responsibility of your children then you are not ready and should not have children." But it is strangely wonderful that with many of us our very own children are the ones who make us more mature. They allow us to experience more fully that which our own parents may have left imcomplete. They awaken within us dormant instincts, dormant selves , even though it may take several children before this happens.

I used to feel greatly resentful toward those who told me, "You'll change when you have children. Your life will change." I felt resentful because I felt threatened. Perhaps I felt threatened that another person was going to control me, change me. I liked the way things were. But children can be the greatest blessing that ever happened to an individual. When one has had children one has had a chance to grow in ways not otherwise possible. Let it not be said, therefore, "You *must* grow. You *must* mature. You must not have children till you are ready." For then we may wait forever. Rather, let it suffice to say, "*Allow* yourself to grow, to mature with your children."

It is through our children that I grew and gained a deeper under-standing of the nature of man, the nature of myself, and of the beauty that life can give. If children can give this to their parents, should we then not reap full the fruit of their being?

Let us, therefore, re-unite the family and say, "our house," "our dining room," "our bedroom." And let us say, "I have respect for you, not only for your things, but for you as a person. I'll be quiet if you want to sleep. I'll rub your back for you. I'll not sprawl my things all over if there is not enough room." This respect has a chance to grow when we live together, not when we are separated behind doors. We learn to live together by doing just that, living together, not by separating.

The newborn baby needs his mother, the toddler needs his mother and father, the young child needs his mother, his father, and his siblings. To be one family, we need to touch and to share. Sleep is so wonderful, let's share it. Let's share it with our loved ones, our children. It was meant to be.

EPILOGUE

Children have slept with their parents since the dawn of mankind, and it is only in the last century that this custom has been called into question as harmful. In this remarkable little book, the first of its kind, Mrs. Thevenin has illustrated how the breakdown in this wholesome, natural custom has come about, and why its restoration is so important to the emotional health and stability of future generations.

The breakdown in family sleeping parallels the alienation, depersonalization and dehumanization that have followed the development of industrialization. Young people have been separated from ancestral homes to flock to the city for jobs, where too often they can be "cogs in a machine," and not even know their next door neighbors.

Women were alienated from their own body processes, anesthesized in labor, separated from their infants at birth. Anesthetics and the accompanying problems necessitated more hospital births, separating the woman and baby from the father. The alienated infant was kept in a room separate from his mother and fed with a bottle. On his return home, the alienation was continued by being put in his "own" bed, often in a separate room.

The trends toward dehumanization continue with the artificial premature severing of mother and infant through widespread abortion, the possibilities of artificial insemination, and the current research toward the development of conception in a test tube and artificial pregnancies in laboratory conditions. It is all too easy for needed research and helpful techniques to become the "norm!" Already there are legal attempts in some nations to control the number of children in a family and mandatory preschool, where children are reared by the state almost from birth.

How greatly we need to return to an outlook which builds relationships, rather than moves toward destroying them! The infant who has slept with his mother for nine months prenatally needs time to be weaned from her presence more gradually; and needs time in which to build a relationship with his father, who has been away at work all day, and needs opportunity to gain confidence in his own fatherhood through the closeness of a sleeping infant.

How much a child is in the parental bed will differ from family to family, and even from child to child. Those of us who have let our children sleep with us have seen them grow into warm, secure, loving adults. Our six children were in and out of the parental bed. But we can really be grateful to Mrs. Thevenin for encouraging mothers and fathers to follow their hearts, rather than the "experts" and know that it is right!

> —*Helen Wessel*
> *Author of* Childbirth and the Family
> *(Harper and Row, 1973)*
> *Edited (with Harlan Ellis, M.D.)* Childbirth
> Without Fear *by the late Grantly Dick-Read*
> *(4th ed. Harper and Row, 1972)*
> *President of Bookmates International, Inc.*

APPENDIX

TWO QUESTIONNAIRES

Following is a resume of the answers of the two questionnaires. Although put in different words, many of the questions received similar answers. I have here given either samples of typical and varied responses or a resume since some questions have been dealt with in the text.

The second questionnaire was sent to those whose first questionnaire seemed to indicate that the parent(s) could assist me in adding depth to the quality of my study. Of the fifty-three that were sent out, forty-seven were returned.

I must emphasize again that these questions were not designed for statistical purposes, but rather to gain insight into the opinions and experiences of those parents who *have* allowed their children to sleep with them. The questions are based on the queries which I received when I talked about co-family sleeping.

Questionnaire No. 1

1. How many children do you have? Ages?

    The number of children ranged from one child to nine children in a family. The ages ranged from two months to twenty-seven years.

2. Why did you allow your child, children, to sleep with you?

    This question is covered in full in the chapter "Why Parents Feel It Was Meant to Be." The two most common answers were: "Because my child seemed to need it," and "after a bad dream."

3. For how long (i.e. every night, for several months after birth, several years, a few hours each night)?

    The most frequent pattern that was mentioned indicated that with each additional child in the family, the parents relaxed restrictions, and the time the child spent in his parents' bed became correspondingly longer. A few parents allowed their first child to sleep with them.

4. Did husband and wife readily agree on this arrangement? (sample responses)

    I felt guilty at first because I thought my husband would object

161

to the lack of privacy. He was a little uneasy at first, but gradually came to like the idea for its naturalness.

Husband was afraid of smothering the child, or of its falling out of bed, but he now lets La Leche League guide him.

Husband was all for it; I was hesitant.

Yes, we both agreed that it would be best for the child.

5. Did it interfere with your sexual relationship?

Some of the outstanding answers are covered in the chapter "Marital Relations." A very few answered "yes" or "sometimes." Most indicated "no," with the explanation that, although it did at times interfere, it did not cause a great deal of concern or friction between either the man and wife, or parents and children.

6. How and when did the child/children begin sleeping in his own bed at all times?

There seems to be an indication that the child who slept with his parents from birth on, was more likely to want to sleep with other members of the family once he outgrew the parental bed. Some children were gently guided away from the parental bed. Others were allowed to make the decision themselves. The ages differed from child to child.

7. What are your experiences of having siblings sleep together?

This question is covered in the "Siblings" chapter. Those parents who had experiences with siblings sleeping together remarked that the children seemed closer than when they had slept in separate rooms. Also, without parental interference, young children seem to seek each other's company at night. (Provided that they are not in the parents' bed).

8. Would you have liked to have your child sleep with you, but refrained from doing so? If yes, why did you decide against it?

Responses to this question are specifically dealt with in the chapter "Why Parents Hesitate."

9. Did the sleeping arrangements vary with each child?

A continuous step-by-step growing toward co-family sleeping was the usual answer to this question.

10. Have you talked about this subject with friends?
(sample answers)

Yes, with La Leche League mothers. Outside LLL, I receive a very cool reception to this idea.

Yes. Although I have found that when the first reaction is usually negative, or questioning, the longer I talk with the person, the more positive the reaction is and frequently some admission is given such as, "I used to sleep with my parents," or "I sure wish I had done it with my children."

Yes, but some people tend to keep it a hush-hush subject.

I am a single parent and sleep with my child for comfort and security. I have found that there are few people with whom I can talk about this matter.

11. Could you give me any experiences or opinions?

I lie down with my children for naps and nighttime, until they have gone to sleep. I find that this half hour of relaxation, even a slight drowsing, gives me a good break and lift. I frequently feel refreshed after this.

With several older children in the family, who now sleep with each other, nighttime is the only time my husband and I can enjoy the baby without interruptions.

If our toddler awoke before my husband and I did in the morning, he never climbed out of bed but was content to lie awake and enjoy himself. We never worried that he would get out of bed by himself without our knowing about it.

I enjoyed it from the beginning because I was always aware of her well-being. Heaven only knows how many times those first three months I awakened and listened for the sound of her breathing.

Once I got used to it, I really enjoyed it.

One morning a few months ago, I was sobered by the thought that our children were really getting older. It had been a couple of months and no one had been in our bed to cuddle with us. It made me very sad to think that maybe we would not be having any more night visitors.

If a child is sleeping with his parents every night and someone, particularly a parent, does not sleep well under such an arrangement and the end result is a very tired parent during the day, then I feel an alternative should be sought.*

I do not feel comfortable with the plan some families have of not providing a bed at all for their children. I feel parental privacy is important. I've always felt free to return a child to his own bed

---

*The author agrees.

if he were too restless, talkative or snoring too loud.

My toddler nurses all night long. (He holds the nipple in his mouth.) A La Leche League counselor suggested that perhaps he was afraid that I would put him back into his own bed, as I indeed used to do when he was through nursing. Perhaps he is holding on because he is afraid of being separated from me.

My babies used nursing and our bed as a means of relaxing and going to sleep for naps and nighttime. I've found with those children of mine (six in all) who gave up nursing, pacifier or bottle before age three or three and a half, that relaxing was much more difficult for them.

My mother did not share our present feelings on this subject when she brought up her children, (during the days when the doctors allowed feedings only every four hours and the children had to sleep through the night in their own cribs, etc). Now, however, she feels our method is "super." She wishes she had used it also. As a result, our "Nanny" sleeps with our children when she cares for them. They love snuggling with her, and she with them.

There is nothing more precious than waking up in the morning and sharing with your husband the wonderful sight of a child as he awakens and smiles at you.

Questionnaire No. 2

11. Did either you or your husband sleep with parents or siblings? At what age? Same bed? Same room?

12. Have you had occasion to sleep close to others (e.g. in camping)?

The indications from the returns of questions eleven and twelve was that it was easier for parents to accept children in their bed who themselves had slept close to someone before they were married, viz. their own parents, siblings, college roommates, or in camping situations, etc., than it was for those who had always slept alone.

13. While your child/children were in your bed, did you talk with your spouse before going to sleep? Did it awaken the child/children? What were the results?

Yes, of course we talked. Children listened. No problems.

Children sleep through our conversations.

We talked to the child too, then we all went to sleep.

14. Have you slept with a child on a water bed?

At first I feared she might get a chill from the bed, so I used extra padding.

My baby tended to roll in between the wooden frame and the waterbed. Since this could be quite serious, I stuffed a blanket in between the frame and bed.

15. Did your child ever have a "bad dream" when he slept in your bed or in a siblings' bed?

Specific answers have been given in the text. The returns seemed to indicate that a child has few, if any, bad dreams when he sleeps with someone else.

16. Many authorities warn mothers against taking children into the family bed when father is away on a trip, lest the child begin to look forward to seeing father leave. Do you agree? What is your experience?

My husband takes many business trips and my children, who sleep with us on and off, are always glad to have him back.

As long as the child sleeps with his parents when Dad is home, it should not matter.

I felt guilty, so I would not permit them to come in when Dad was away.

My husband sometimes has to work nights. I try to treat my children exactly the same as I would any other night.

I have never found my daughter eager to see her father leave so she can sleep with me.

17. Have you noticed a difference in the sleeping positions of your baby when he(she) sleeps alone vs. when he(she) sleeps with you?

This is covered in the chapter "The Infant."

18. Several people have asked me what to do about sexual relations when children sleep with parents. What suggestions do you have?

We usually have sex in another room—living room, den, vacant bedroom.

We've usually had an hour or two before the children joined us in bed.

We move the sleeping child to the floor (on a pad) or to another bedroom.

(See also chapter on "Marital Relations.")

19. Do you find yourself less anxious for the child to sleep through

the night when he sleeps with you?

Definitely YES. When I am asked, "Does your baby sleep through the night yet?" I find myself saying, "Well, yes, because he sleeps with me, and when he does awaken he nurses and we both resume sleep." I wonder if that makes sense to most people. The same applies to our toddlers and preschoolers if they are in bed with us. We sometimes don't remember if they were awake or not during the night because our sleep was interrupted so slightly.

I don't even expect my children to sleep through the night. That realization alone has made life easier for me. Why fight it?

When it does begin to bother me, it helps me to check what I have been eating. I have found that if I eat too much unnutritious food, I become irritable and start taking things personally, even the baby's waking at night.

20. A nursing child may nurse more when he(she) sleeps with you. Does this bother you?

It did not bother me since I could resume sleep immediately.

Occasionally when he goes through a restless time and nurses off and on for a long time. But I think he could also be getting a parent up and down a lot if he were in a different bed these times.

Yes, when I am very tired.

No bother. It's a fine pacifier in the night and everyone gets more sleep.

I have not found my baby to nurse more when he sleeps with me.

21. If you have a foster or adopted child, please answer the following question: Do you feel it is valuable to allow him or her to sleep with you and your husband in your bed? Why? On what occasions has this child slept with you?

This question is dealt with in the chapter on "The Adopted Child."

22. Please comment on problems you have encountered and the solutions you have found useful concerning children in the parental bed.

Outside of "I wish we had a bigger bed," few parents answered this question. This at first puzzled me. But then it became clear: Many parents do not find it to be a problem to have their children sleep with them.

23. What interesting and/or unusual occurrences have taken place in your family situation which would add interest to this study?

A husband offered these comments: It is comical! At least the child is with you and you're not worrying about him. If you are having a family you have to expect to make allowances. Nothing hinders your sex life—where there is a will there is a way. I used to get kicked a lot and for a while I wasn't getting enough sleep. But the child finally learned to sleep on his own part of the bed.

I'll never forget waking up one morning shortly after our third child was born and discovering that I had spent the night in the same bed with my squished husband, my nursing baby, the other two kids, AND our big Irish Setter—which wouldn't be so bad except that our bed is just a small double bed, nothing fancy.

Our biggest mistake was to buy bunk beds for our boys. A double bed would have been cheaper and more comfortable since they sleep together anyway.

REACTIONS TO THE BOOK

During the first year that the book has been in print, I have received a great many letters from parents, doctors, child educators and others, which all attest with overwhelming enthusiasm to the need for THE FAMILY BED. Many of these letters are extremely touching and moving, with an almost constant admission of relief from guilt, and a welcome acceptance of my faith in parents.

Some may not agree with the concept of this book, but it can no longer be ignored that co-family sleeping *does* go on in our society, and that it *does* have a positive effect on the family. I find myself in a unique position because I am receiving many letters which attest to this fact. In this second enlarged edition I have enclosed excerpts from letters which I have received during this first year.

• • •

THE FAMILY BED should be required reading for all parents, all expectant parents, all pediatricians, and all child guidance experts contemplating writing anything directed at parents. You have put childrearing into the perspective it has needed to be put into ever since the first expert attempted to tell a mother how to do her mothering.—Shirley L. Radl, author MOTHER'S DAY IS OVER

Your book is a living Bible. I was so inspired and moved by it, I can truly say it ranks with the top few *most* influential books of this century!—Alice Bricklin, author MOTHERLOVE

I'm reading THE FAMILY BED for the second time. It is so warm and informative. Parts of it hit too close to home and make me feel like crying, and other parts make me feel good all over.—Minnesota

I've recently come across THE FAMILY BED and I must admire your courage in speaking a great truth that appears at first glance so strange and contrary.—California

Before we had even finished reading THE FAMILY BED it was apparent it would be in our "where were you when we needed you?" list.—Iowa

169

I have just completed reading your book. It was superb. I was not able to put it down until I had finished it. I am a P.E.T. instructor and have already introduced the book to my colleagues where it won great approval.—Ontario, Canada

My heart is filled with gratitude. THE FAMILY BED has allowed me to get rid of my guilt. Guilt I had because I didn't want to make my babies cry through the night. Guilt I had because I did not believe my babies were devious plotters to keep me from my rights to sleep alone, undisturbed with their father.—U.S.

How refreshing it was to read THE FAMILY BED. In a society which consciously and subconsciously strives to separate parents and children from birth through all stages of development, Mrs. Thevenin dares to try to reunite them. Sometimes it is hard to fulfill a young child's insatiable needs. This book gives us the courage and strength to continue.—H.O.M.E. Leader Esther Herman

Thank you for writing this marvelous book, it is the best I have read in years! You have given expression and support to many of my deepest feelings about motherhood and family. A fantastic book!—Maryland

Thank you for writing this book! No more guilt!!!—California

I was told that I was "sick" and probably had a deep down "*lust*" for my children. With your book I hope people's views will change somewhat.—U.S.

Our son usually sleeps in his own bed which is in our room, but sometimes, at 2 or 3 a.m. we hear a quiet, very polite voice saying, "Daddy, pssst, Daddy, can I sleep in your bed?", and then we wake up one happy, loving family.—U.S.

I cannot express in words the gratitude I feel towards you for this book. May God bless you and your family always.—California

Thank you for writing this book. I thought I was the only person in the world whose kids slept with them, (and ashamed to tell anyone).—Maryland

This book is great! It has us sleeping together again, and happier, smiles in the morning again.—U.S.

THE FAMILY BED is the title of an excellent and thought provoking book. Although I have always recommended parents to go immediately to their crying children, I used to advise against bringing them into their own beds. My advice now is that if it is clear that the child is too frightened to go to sleep on his own, no harm will result from bringing him into the parental bed. Psychoanalysts may be firm in their advice that parents must never allow their children into their beds, but those who have practiced it know better and have not had any dire consequences to face—just the opposite. A giant sized family bed could be the best wedding present for future family peace and enjoyment.—Dr. Hugh Jolly, The London Times, England

Our son who is four, always had sleep problems. He walked in his sleep. He had bad dreams. He would urinate in the strangest places, or he would wet the bed. He also screamed and yelled at night for fear of monsters. Now he has been sleeping with his 6 year old sister, and his problems have practically vanished.—U.S.

THE FAMILY BED is fantastic, beautifully and warmly written. I hope it can start a trend in our society back to more natural ways of raising families.—U.S.

Thank you for the book. Now I feel as if a big weight has been lifted from my heart.—Ohio

When I need medical advice, I'll go to Dr. Spock. When I'm confused about how to care for my children, I'll go to THE FAMILY BED.—Illinois

I remember being scared at night and wanting to sleep with my parents, but I was always ushered back to my own room. So I always went back and did the next best thing. I took my blanket and pillow and slept on the floor next to my mother's side of the bed. After reading your book I became convinced that co-family sleeping is the only way to raise children. You've taught one more person in the world how to raise children a little more humanely. Thank you.—U.S.

When my wife and I were first married we purchased an old antique bed. As time went on within our first year of marriage we had a son. My parents graciously offered to purchase the traditional crib, which they said was "essential." So our son spent his first 9 months there. One night while my wife and I were in bed, the antiquity of our bed finally caught up with time and completely broke apart. We then decided to just use the box spring and mattress. I found this to be a blessing later when my wife began to bring our son into the bed with us. He would not fall out of bed because it was so close to the ground. I'm really glad that our old bed came crashing down and I hope that the tradition of "cribbing" children also tumbles down, as it is the case with antique beds and old traditions that no longer serve a worthwhile purpose.—Illinois

We are now a much happier and closer family. We are all together and Daddy feels much more involved and closer to the baby.—North Carolina

During my hospital stay I was walking through a corridor, when I met an Oriental mother crying because her child was being operated on. I consoled her as best I could and when I went back in the afternoon to inquire about the child, I was moved to see her inside the hospital bed with her 4 year old child, both of them asleep peacefully.—Mexico

Our eight year old stopped sleeping with us, by himself, several months ago. He comes once in a while now. He would not stop when we tried to make him.—Kentucky

All of this nonsense about flame-retardant sleepware is unnecessary when everybody is in the same room!—California

I am only 18 right now, but am very interested in the whole childrearing experience. I hope to have a large family of my own, someday. Your book and the whole concept within it are so special I feel that there couldn't possibly be anything more positive or right for everyone concerned.— Pennsylvania

We were already settled in our co-family sleeping when we read your book, but it reinforced what we had already experienced.—U.S.

Our children had no physical or psychological problems. We simply had a hassle, a real hassle at bed time and all were very tired, making tempers flare easily. It was one request after another, up and down, up and down, not really a nice end to the day for parent or child. We are all happier now, and I'd start sooner with a next child.—Illinois

Cribs and playpens encourage premature standing and walking; the baby, in an attempt to get out, pulls her/himself up, into the upright position before Nature intended; that is, before the lumbar curve of the spine has been formed. The result is a great deal of muscular tension and armoring,

172

putting stress on the skeletal system. This is probably one of the reasons so many adults suffer from lower back pain.—U.S.

After we read your book we told our six year old son, not only can you come into our bed, but you are *welcome* in our bed; it's FINE for you to come in; there's nothing at all wrong about your coming in. WELCOME, WELCOME, WELCOME dear sweet child. He was so beautiful, lovingly touched and thrilled. His nighttime terrors, nightmares, loneliness, fretfulness and rejection vanished almost instantly. He now feels safe, loved and wanted. I so applaud your book for finally bringing this essential, tremendously neglected area of child care out in the open. And I thank you very deeply on behalf of my whole family for bringing back peace and sanity, love and comfort, natural warmth and trust and security and family togetherness to our nighttime.—Washington, D.C.

ABOUT THE AUTHOR

Tine Thevenin was born in the Netherlands and educated there and in the United States. She has lived in this country twenty years. She comes from a musical family and has, herself, performed professionally on the flute. She is married to a musician with the Minneapolis Symphony Orchestra.

Mrs. Thevenin is the mother of two children and has been, for a number of years, a counselor for La Leche League, an organization committed to a belief in the importance of good mothering through breastfeeding.

Mrs. Thevenin strongly feels that the strength of this book should lie in the fact that it was written by a mother; and mothering, she believes, is a special profession which can only be learned at home, with children.

Recommended Reading List

BREAST-FEEDING AND NATURAL CHILD SPACING by Sheila Kippley

INSOMNIA by Gay G. Luce and Dr. Julius Segal.

TOUCHING: The Human Siginificance of the Skin by Ashley Montagu

PARENT EFFECTIVENESS TRAINING by Thomas Gordon

THE WOMANLY ART OF BREASTFEEDING, La Leche League
  Manual

La Leche League Reprints:
  Nursing the New Born. . .How Soon?
  Frequent Night Nursing of Toddler and Clinging Dependence
    During the Day.
  Thoughts About Weaning.
  When Baby's Crying Becomes Trying.

LLL Newsletter from 1970 to present. (Articles on sleep.)

Table Of References

Cover quote: LLL NEWS, 1971, p. 3.

The Sources

1—PSYCHOLOGY TODAY, Newton, N. "Breastfeeding," Jn. 1968.

Why Some Parents Hesitate

1—Salk, Lee. WHAT EVERY CHILD WOULD LIKE HIS PARENTS TO KNOW. N.Y. McKay Comp. Inc. 1972, p. 106.

2—"Infant Care." Children's Bureau Publ. No. 8, 1967, U.S. Dept. of Health, Educ., and Welfare, Wash. D.C. p. 25.

3—Brazelton, T. Berry. INFANTS AND MOTHERS. N.Y. Dell Publ. 1969, p. 9.

4—Ibid.

5—Janov, Arthur. THE PRIMAL SCREAM. N.Y. Dell Publ. 1970.

6—"What's A Mother To Do?" NEWSWEEK. Sept. 23, 1968. p. 68.

7—Spock, Benjamin. BABY AND CHILD CARE. N.Y. Pocket Books. 1968. p. 169.

8—Ibid. p. 196

9—Ibid. p. 355

10—Luce, Gay, and Segal, Julius. INSOMNIA. Garden City, N.Y. Doubleday and Comp. 1969. p. 197.

11—Ibid p. XI.

12—Gersh, Marvin J. HOW TO RAISE CHILDREN AT HOME IN YOUR SPARE TIME. Greenwich, Conn. Fawcett Publ., Inc. 1966. p. 74.

13—"Ear Infection." CEAN TODAY. Aug. 1973. P.O. Box 20091, Minneapolis, Minn. 55420. p. 73.

14—"Facts About Sudden Infant Death Syndrome." National Foundation for Sudden Infant Death, 1501 Broadway, N.Y. 10036. 1970. p. 9.

15—Gerard, Alice. PLEASE BREASTFEED YOUR BABY. New American Library. Pocket Book. 1970. p. 97.

16—Combe, A. MANAGEMENT OF INFANCY. N.Y. Fowlers and Wells. 1840. p. 207.

17—"Facts About Sudden Infant Death Syndrome." NFSID, 1501 Broadway, N.Y. 10036. 1970. p. 4.

18—Duluth, Minn. Newspaper. (Name of newspaper and date unknown.)

19—"Facts About Sudden Infant Death Syndrome." NFSID, 1501 Broadway, N.Y. 10036. 1970, p. 4.

20—"Crib Deaths." LLL NEWS. Franklin Park, Ill., 1971. p. 89.

22—Aldrich, C. Anderson. BABIES ARE HUMAN BEINGS. p. 85.

23—"Facts About Sudden Infant Death Syndrome." NFSID, 1501 Broadway, N.Y. 1970. p. 5.

24—La Leche League International. THE WOMANLY ART OF BREASTFEEDING. 9616 Minneapolis Ave., Franklin Park, Ill. 60131. 1958. p. 83.

The Importance of Sleeping Together

1—Montagu, Ashley. TOUCHING. N.Y. Columbia Univ. Press. 1971. p. 79.

2—Montagu, Ashley. MAN: HIS FIRST MILLION YEARS. Mentor Book, N.Y. 1957. p. 88.

3—Montagu, Ashley. ON BEING HUMAN. N.Y. Hawthorn Books. 1966. p. 93.

4—Montagu, Ashley. MAN: HIS FIRST MILLION YEARS. Mentor Book, N.Y. 1957. p. 88.

5—Salk, Lee and Kramer, Rita. HOW TO RAISE A HUMAN BEING. N.Y. Random House. 1969. p. 14.

6—Ratner, H. "Public Health Aspect of Breastfeeding." Section on pediatrics. Jn. 25, 1958. American Medical Association Annual Meeting. San Francisco, Ca. Distributed by LLLI, Franklin Park, Ill. 60131. p. 3.

7—Salk, Lee. WHAT EVERY CHILD WOULD LIKE HIS PARENTS TO KNOW. N.Y. McKay Comp. 1972. p. 1.

8—Janov, Arthur. THE PRIMAL SCREAM. N.Y. Dell Publ. 1970. p. 27.

9—Montagu, Ashley "Some Factors in Family Cohesion." PSYCHIATRY, Vol. 7. 1944. p. 349.

10—Montagu, Ashley. ON BEING HUMAN. N.Y. Hawthorn Books, 1966. p. 96.

11—Ibid.

12—"Waiting Game vs. Gaining Weight." LLLI reprint. LLLI, Franklin Park, Ill. p. 1.

13—Montagu, Ashley. "Some Factors in Family Cohesion." PSYCHIATRY, Vol. 7. 1944. p. 350.

14—Ibid.

15—Montagu, Ashley. TOUCHING. Columbia Univ. Press. N.Y. 1971. p. 22.

16—NATIONAL GEOGRAPHIC MAG. Aug. 1972. p. 244.

17—Montagu, Ashley. TOUCHING. Columbia Univ. Press. N.Y. 1971. p. 247.

18—Ibid p. 4.

19—Ratcliff, J.D. "I'm Joe's Skin." READERS' DIGEST. 1972. p. 114.

20—Montagu, Ashley. TOUCHING. Columbia Univ. Press. N.Y. 1971. p. 80.

21—Kenny, James and Schreiter, Robert "Of Babies, Beds and Teddy Bears." MARRIAGE MAGAZINE. Jan. 1971. p. 18-24.

22—Richardson, S.A. et al. CHILDBEARING: ITS SOCIAL AND PSYCHOLOGICAL ASPECTS. Williams and Wilkens. 1967. p. 177.

23—Ibid p. 186.

24—Ibid p. 179.

25—Ibid.

26—Kenny, J. and Schreiter, R. "Of Babies, Beds and Teddy Bears." MARRIAGE MAGAZINE. Jan. 1971. p. 21.

27—Richardson, S.A. et al. CHILDREARING: ITS SOCIAL AND PSYCHOLOGICAL ASPECTS. Williams and Wilkens. 1967. p. 181.

28—Montagu, Ashley. TOUCHING. Columbia Univ. Press. N.Y. 1971. p. 287.

29—Ibid p. 120.

30—Ibid p. 159.

31—Luce, Gay and Segal, Julius. INSOMNIA. Garden City, N.Y. Doubleday and Comp. 1969. p. 163.

32—Bowlby, John. ATTACHMENT AND LOSS, Vol. 2: SEPARATION. Basic Books. 1973. p. 166-168.

33—Ibid p. 167.

34—Luce, Gay and Segal, Julius. SLEEP. Coward-McGann Inc. N.Y. 1966. p. 25.

35—Luce, Gay and Segal, Julius. INSOMNIA. Garden City, N.Y. Doubleday and Comp. 1969. p. 20.

36—Froehlich, Edwina. La Leche League of Minnesota, Third State Seminar Transcript. April, 1972. LLLI, Franklin Park, Ill. 60131.

37—Chisholm, Brock. PRESCRIPTION FOR SURVIVAL. Columbia Univ. Press. N.Y. 1957. p. 40.

38—Salk, Lee. WHAT EVERY CHILD WOULD LIKE HIS PARENTS TO KNOW. N.Y. McKay Comp. 1972. p. 14.

39—Montagu, Ashley. TOUCHING. Columbia Univ. Press. N.Y. 1971. p. 173.

40—Ribble, Margaret. THE RIGHTS OF INFANTS. Columbia Univ. Press. N.Y. 1965. p. 53.

41—Arnstein, Helene. "How Babies Learn To Wait." PARENTS' MAG. Dec. 1970.

42—Morris, Desmond. INTIMATE BEHAVIOR. Random House. N.Y. 1971. p. 103.

Need vs. Habit

1—Salk, Lee. "Role of the Heartbeat in the Relationship Between Mother and Infant." SCIENTIFIC AMERICAN. May, 1973. p. 29.

2—Montagu, Ashley. TOUCHING. Columbia Univ. Press. N.Y. 1971. p. 289.

3—Janov, Arthur. THE PRIMAL SCREAM. Dell Publ. N.Y. 1970. p. 22.

4—"What Is A Mother To Do?" NEWSWEEK. Sept. 23, 1968. p. 69.

5—Hymes, James. CHILD UNDER SIX. Englewood Cliffs, N.J. Prentice Hall. 1963. p. 87.

6—Salk, Lee. WHAT EVERY CHILD WOULD LIKE HIS PARENTS TO KNOW. N.Y. McKay Comp. 1972. p. 42.

7—"Frequent Night Nursing of Toddlers and Clinging Dependence During the Day." LLL reprint No. 77. LLLI, Franklin Park, Ill. 60131. p. 3.

Brief History of Childhood and Sleeping Customs

1—Luce, Gay and Segal, Julius. SLEEP. N.Y. Coward-McGann. 1966. p. 24.

2—Aries. P. CENTURIES OF CHILDHOOD. N.Y. Knopf. 1962. p. 33.

3—Ibid p. 34.

4—Ryerson, Alice. "Medical Advice on Child Rearing 1550-1900." HARVARD ED. REVIEW. Vol. 31. No. 3. p. 313.

5—Aries, P. CENTURIES OF CHILDHOOD. N.Y. Knopf. 1962. p. 34.

6—Ibid p. 106.

7—Ibid p. 394.

8—Luce, Gay and Segal, Julius. INSOMNIA. Garden City, N.Y. Doubleday and Comp. 1969. p. 152.

9—Kenny and Schreiter, "Of Babies, Beds and Teddy Bears." MARRIAGE MAGAZINE. Jan. 1971. p. 22.

10—Aries, P. CENTURIES OF CHILDHOOD. N.Y. Knopf. 1962. p. 103.

11—Ibid p. 106.

12—Ryerson, Alice. "Medical Advice on Child Rearing 1550-1900." HARVARD ED. REVIEW. Vol. 3l, No. 3. p. 302.

13—Aries, P. CENTURIES OF CHILDHOOD. N.Y. Knopf. 1962. p. 115.

14—Ibid p. 412.

15—Ibid p. 400.

16—DeWees, W. TREATISE ON THE PHYSICAL AND MEDICAL TREATMENT OF CHILDREN. Philadelphia, Carey, Lea and Carey. 1829.

17—Stiles, H. BUNDLING. Albany Knickerbocker Publ. 1871. p. 106.

18—Ibid p. 2.

19—Ibid p. 65.

20—Kenny and Schreiter. "Of Babies, Beds and Teddy Bears." MARRIAGE MAGAZINE. Jan. 1971. p. 22.

21—Langer, L. and Langer, A. "The Pursuit of Happiness." (An American Comedy) N.Y. Samuel French. 1934. p. xxvii.

22—Stiles, H. BUNDLING. Albany Knickerbocker Publ. 1871. p. 65.

23—Ryerson, Alice. "Medical Advice on Child Rearing 1550-1900." HARVARD ED. REVIEW. Vol. 31, No. 3. p. 302.

24—Stiles, H. BUNDLING. Albany Knickerbocker Publ. 1871. p. 79.

25—Ryerson, Alice. "Medical Advice on Child Rearing 1550-1900." HARVARD ED. REVIEW. Vol. 31, No. 3. p. 302.

26—Ibid.

27—Luce, Gay and Segal, Julius. INSOMNIA. Garden City, N.Y. Doubleday and Comp. 1969. p. 153.

28—"What Is A Mother To Do?" NEWSWEEK. Sept. 23, 1968. p. 68.

29—LLL of Minnesota, 3rd State Seminar, April 1972. Wessel, Helen. Available through LLLI, Franklin Park,Ill. 60131.

30—"What Is A Mother To Do?" NEWSWEEK. Sept. 23, 1968. p. 68.

31—Nichols, J. SAFE COUNSEL. Chicago, Ill. Franklin Publ. 1928. p. 132.

—Holt, L. Emmett, Jr. CARE AND FEEDING OF CHILDREN. N.Y. Appleton-Century Comp. 1943. p. 20.

32—Kenny and Schreiter. "Of Babies, Beds and Teddy Bears." MARRIAGE MAGAZINE. Jan. 1971. p. 23.

33—Luce, Gay and Segal, J. INSOMNIA. Garden City, N.Y. Doubleday and Comp. 1969. p. 155.

34—Newton, N. FAMILY BOOK OF CHILD CARE. N.Y. Harper and Row. 1957. p. 156.

—CHILD AND FAMILY Quarterly (see general index of magazine) Ed. Herbert Ratner, M.D., Box 508, Oak Park, Ill. 60303.

Some Anthropological Observations

1—Airola, Paavo. ARE YOU CONFUSED?

2—Erickson, Erik. CHILDHOOD AND SOCIETY. N.Y. Norton and Comp. 1963. p. 112.

3—Ford, Clellan and Beach, F. PATTERNS OF SEXUAL BEHAVIOR. N.Y. Harper and Row. 1951. p. 6.

4—Hass, Hans. THE HUMAN ANIMAL. N.Y. Putnam's Sons. 1970.

5—Elkin, A. P. THE AUSTRALIAN ABORIGINES: HOW TO UNDERSTAND THEM. London. 1945.

—Thomas, Elizabeth M. THE HARMLESS PEOPLE. N.Y. Knopf. 1959.

6—Kenny and Schreiter. "Of Babies, Beds and Teddy Bears." MARRIAGE MAGAZINE. Jan. 1971. p. 18.

7—Barry, H. III and Paxson, L. M. "Infancy and Early Childhood: Cross-Cultural Codes 2" ETHNOLOGY. Vol. 10, Oct. 1971.

8—Moloney, James. FEAR: CONTAGION AND CONQUEST. p. 72-84.

9—Montagu, Ashley. TOUCHING. Columbia Univ. Press. N.Y. 1971. p. 117.

10—Ibid p. 249.

—Luce, Gay and Segal, Julius. SLEEP. Coward-McGann. N.Y. 1966. p. 25.

—Johnston, Madeline "Discipline or Indulgence?" PARENTS' MAG. July 1969.

11—Breetveld, J. "Mother and Child in Africa." PSYCHOLOGY TODAY. Feb. 1972. p. 63.

12—Montagu, Ashley. TOUCHING. Columbia Univ. Press. N.Y. 1971. p. 225,233.

13—Montagu, Ashley. ON BEING HUMAN. N.Y. Hawthorn Books. 1966. p. 86.

14—Mead, Margaret. FROM THE SOUTH SEAS. N.Y. Morrow. 1939.

The Infant

1—Montagu, Ashley. "Some Factors in Family Cohesion." PSYCHIATRY. Vol. 7, 1944. p. 351.

2—Montagu, Ashley. TOUCHING. Columbia Univ. Press. N.Y. 1971. p. 65.

3—Ibid.

4—Newton, Niles. MATERNAL EMOTIONS. N.Y. Medical Book Dept. of Harper and Row. 1955. p. 7.

5—Salk, Lee and Kramer, R. HOW TO RAISE A HUMAN BEING. N.Y. Random House. 1969. p. 7.

6—Ibid p. 54.
  —Salk, Lee. WHAT EVERY CHILD WOULD LIKE HIS PARENTS TO KNOW. McKay Comp. N.Y. 1972. p. 6.

7—Albrecht, R. LLL of Minnesota Third State Seminar Transcript. April 1972. Available through LLLI, Franklin Park, Ill. 60131.

8—Brecher, R. "Why Some Mothers Reject Their Babies." REDBOOK. May, 1966. p. 49.

9—"On Nursing the Newborn. . .How Soon?" LLL reprint. LLLI, Franklin Park, Ill. 60131. 1972.

10—Pryor, Karen. NURSING YOUR BABY. N.Y. Pocket Books. 1973. p. 75.

11—"On Nursing the Newborn. . .How Soon?" LLL reprint. LLLI, Franklin Park, Ill. 60131. 1972.

12—Ibid.

13—Haire, Doris. THE CULTURAL WARPING OF CHILDBIRTH. ICEA. Doris B. Haire, 251 Nottingham Way. Hillside, N.J. 1972. p. 27.
  —Albrecht, R. "Prepared Childbirth in Hospital." LLL of Minnesota Third State Seminar Transcript. April 1972.

14—Ribble, M. THE RIGHTS OF INFANTS. Columbia Univ. Press N.Y. 1965. p. 18.

15—Montagu, A. TOUCHING. Columbia Univ. Press. N.Y. 1971. p. 90.

—Marlow, D. TEXTBOOK OF PEDIATRIC NURSING. Phil. Saunders Comp. 1969. p. 102.

—Ziegel, Erna and V. Blarcom C. OBSTETRIC NURSING. N.Y. McMillan Comp. 1972. p. 575.

16—Fuller, J. 2,000,000,000 GUINEA PIGS. N.Y. Putnam. 1972. p. 264.

17—Ibid.

18—Haire, D. THE CULTURAL WARPING OF CHILDBIRTH. ICEA. Doris B. Haire, 251 Nottingham Way, Hillside, N.J. 1972.

19—Ibid p. 7.

20—"On Nursing The Newborn...How Soon?" LLL reprint. LLLI, Fanklin Park, Ill. 60131. 1972. p. 3.

21—Montagu, Ashley. TOUCHING. Columbia Univ. Press. N.Y. 1971. p. 114.

22—Pryor, K. NURSING YOUR BABY. N.Y. Pocket Books. 1973. p. 46.

23—LLL NEWS. Franklin Park, Ill. 60131. 1970. p. 70.

24—Janov, A. THE FEELING CHILD. N.Y. Simon and Schuster. 1973. p. 27.

25—Kenny and Schreiter. "Of Babies, Beds and Teddy Bears." MARRIAGE MAGAZINE. Jan. 1971. p. 18.

26—Salk, Lee. "Role of the Heartbeat in the Relationship Between Mother and Infant." SCIENTIFIC AMERICAN. May, 1973. p. 29.

27—Salk, Lee and Kramer, R. HOW TO RAISE A HUMAN BEING. N.Y. Random House. 1969. p. 65.

28—Spock, B. BABY AND CHILD CARE. N.Y. Pocket Books. 1968. p. 186.

29—Richardson, S. A. et al. CHILDBEARING: ITS SOCIAL AND PSYCHOLOGICAL ASPECTS. Williams and Wilkens. 1967. p. 183.

30—Bowlby, J. ATTACHMENT AND LOSS: Vol. 2. SEPARATION. Basic Books. 1973.

31—Salk, Lee and Kramer, R. HOW TO RAISE A HUMAN BEING. N.Y. Ramdom House. 1969. p. 65.

32—Morris, D. INTIMATE BEHAVIOR. N.Y. Random House. 1971. p. 19.

33—Perkins, J. "Possible Causes of Crying and Frequent Nighttime Nursings." Minneapolis, Minn. 1972.

34—Morris, D. INTIMATE BEHAVIOR. N.Y. Random House, 1971. p. 25.

35—LLL NEWS. Illinois Insert. March, 1973.

36—Luce, Gay and Segal, Julius. INSOMNIA. Garden City, N.Y. Doubleday Corp. 1969.

37—Ibid p. 245.

38—Ibid.

39—THE WOMANLY ART OF BREASTFEEDING. LLL Manual. LLLI, Franklin Park, Ill. 60131. 1958. p. 61.

40—LLL NEWS. Minnesota Insert. Vol. 15, No. 2. 1973.

41—Lorenz. KING SOLOMON'S RING. N.Y. Coward-McGann, Inc. 1952.

The Child Past Infancy

1—Montagu, Ashley. TOUCHING. Columbia Univ. Press. N.Y. 1971. p. 253.

2—Kenny and Schreiter. "Of Babies, Beds and Teddy Bears." MARRIAGE MAGAZINE. Jan. 1971. p. 23.

3—Montagu, Ashley. TOUCHING. Columbia Univ. Press. N.Y. 1971. p. 253.

4—Newton, Niles. FAMILY BOOK OF CHILD CARE. N.Y. Harper and Row. 1957. p. 187.

5—Ibid p. 185.

6—Ibid p. 188.

7—Kenny and Schreiter. "Of Babies, Beds and Teddy Bears." MARRIAGE MAGAZINE. Jan. 1971. p. 23.

8—Bowlby, J. ATTACHMENT AND LOSS, Vol. 2: SEPARATION. Basic Books. 1973. p. 190.

9—Ibid p. 115, 118.

10—Luce, Gay and Segal, Julius. INSOMNIA. Garden City, N.Y. Doubleday and Comp. 1969. p. 163.

11—Ibid p. 159.

Siblings

1—Chisholm, Brock. PRESCRIPTION FOR SURVIVAL. N.Y. Columbia Univ. Press. 1957. p. 10.

2—Spock, B. BABY AND CHILD CARE. Pocket Books. N.Y. 1968. p. 169.

3—Salk, Lee. WHAT EVERY CHILD WOULD LIKE HIS PARENTS TO KNOW. N.Y. McKay Comp. 1972. p. 14.

Marital Relations

1—Prescott, James W. "Cross-Cultural Studies." HEW, Growth and 'Development Branch, National Institute of Child Health and Human Development, Bethesda, Md. 20014.

2—Ibid.

3—Janov, A. THE PRIMAL SCREAM. N.Y. Simon and Schuster. 1973.

4—Ford, C. and Beach, F. PATTERNS OF SEXUAL BEHAVIOR. N.Y. Harper and Row. 1951. p. 2.

5—Newton, Niles.

6—Ford, C. and Beach, F. PATTERNS OF SEXUAL BEHAVIOR. N.Y. Harper and Row. 1951. p. 190.

7—Ibid p. 189.

8—Ibid p. 68.

9—Ibid p. 2.

10—Gersh, M. HOW TO RAISE CHILDREN AT HOME IN YOUR SPARE TIME. Greenwich, Conn. Fawcett Publ. Inc. 1966.

11—Ryerson, Alice. "Medical Advice on Child Rearing 1550-1900." HARVARD ED. REVIEW. Vol. 31, No. 3. p. 302.

12—Ibid.

13—Bowlby, J. ATTACHMENT AND LOSS. Vol. 2: SEPARATION. Basic Books. 1973 p. 29.

14—Ibid.

15—Ibid.

16—U.S. NEWS AND WORLD REPORT. Oct. 1975. p. 32.

17—Luce, Gay and Segal, J. INSOMNIA. Garden City, N.Y. Doubleday and Comp. 1969. p. 163.

18—Krebs. "Interruptus." PSYCHOLOGY TODAY. Jan. 1970. p. 153.

19—Cutler, Lucy. Minneapolis, Minn. 1973.

The Adopted Child

1—Hormann, Elizabeth. RELACTATION: A GUIDE TO BREAST-FEEDING THE ADOPTED BABY. Mrs. Karl H. Hormann, 1 Merrill Ave., Belmont, Mass. 1971. p. 12.

Hospitalization of a Member of the Family

1—Salk, Lee and Kramer, Rita. HOW TO RAISE A HUMAN BEING. N.Y. Random House. 196ᵒ. ҏ. 13.

Nighttime Is For Sleeping

1—Luce, Gay and Segal, Julius. INSOMNIA. Garden City, N.Y. Doubleday and Comp. 1969. p. 162.

Conclusion

1—Montagu, Ashley. ON BEING HUMAN. N.Y. Hawthorn Books. 1966. p. 91.

2—Benedict, Ruth. PATTERNS OF CULTURE. Boston. Houghton, Mifflin. 1934.

3—Bowlby, John. ATTACHMENT AND LOSS, Vol. 2: SEPARATION. Basic Books. 1973.

4—Montagu, Ashley. ON BEING HUMAN. N.Y. Hawthorn Books. l966. p. 111.

5—Packard, Vance. THE SEXUAL WILDERNESS. N.Y. McKay Comp. 1968. p. 33.

BIBLIOGRAPHY

Books

Airola, Paavo, ARE YOU CONFUSED, Paavo Publ. P.O. Box 22001, Phoenix, Ariz. 1971.

Aldrich, C. Anderson, and Mary Aldrich, BABIES ARE HUMAN BEINGS

Aries, Philippe, CENTURIES OF CHILDHOOD, N.Y. Alfred A. Knopf. 1962.

Baker, Carlos, ERNEST HEMINGWAY, N.Y. Scribner's Sons, 1969.

Bates, Marston and Abbott, Donald, CORAL ISLAND, N.Y. Scribner's Sons. 1958.

Benedict, Ruth, PATTERNS OF CULTURE, Boston, Houghton-Mifflin. 1934.

BIBLE, Red Letter Edition, Book Inc. Publ. Boston, Mass.

Bowlby, John, ATTACHMENT AND LOSS, Vol. 2: SEPARATION, Basic Books. 1973.

Brazelton, Berry, INFANTS AND MOTHERS, N.Y. Dell Publ. Comp. Inc. 1969.

Cava, Esther Laden, THE COMPLETE QUESTION AND ANSWER BOOK OF CHILD TRAINING, N.Y. Hawthorn Book Inc. 1972.

Chavasse, H., ADVICE TO A WIFE, N.Y. American News Comp. 1878.

Chisholm, Brock, PRESCRIPTION FOR SURVIVAL, N.Y. Columbia Univ. Press. 1957.

Clymer, Swinburne, THE MYSTERY OF SEX AND RACE REGEN-ERATION, Quakertown, Penn. Philosophical Publ. Comp. 1902.

Combe, A. MANAGEMENT OF INFANCY. N.Y. Fowlers and Wells. 1840.

DeWees, W. TREATISE ON THE PHYSICAL AND MEDICAL TREATMENT OF CHILDREN, Philadelphia, Carey, Lea and Carey. 1829.

Elkin, A. O. THE AUSTRALIAN ABORIGINES: HOW TO UNDER-STAND THEM, London, Angus and Robertson Ltd. 1945.

191

English, Spurgeon O. and Pearson, G. EMOTIONAL PROBLEMS OF LIVING.

Erickson, Erik, CHILDHOOD AND SOCIETY, N.Y. W. W. Norton and Comp. 1963.

Ford, Clellan and Beach, Frank, PATTERNS OF SEXUAL BEHAVIOR, N.Y. Harper and Row, 1951.

Fraiberg, Selma, THE MAGIC YEARS, N.Y. Scribner's Sons. 1959.

Fuller, John, 2,000,000,000 GUINEA PIGS, N.Y. Putnam. 1972.

Gathorne-Hardy, T., THE UNNATURAL HISTORY OF THE NANNY Dial Press. New York, 1973.

Gerard, Alice, PLEASE BREASTFEED YOUR BABY, N.Y. New American Library. Pocket Book. 1970.

Gersch, Marvin, HOW TO RAISE CHILDREN AT HOME IN YOUR SPARE TIME, Greenwich, Conn. Fawcett Publ., Inc. 1966.

Greenberg, J. IN THIS SIGN, Avon Books, 1972.

Haire, Doris, THE CULTURAL WARPING OF CHILDBIRTH, ICEA, Doris B. Haire, 251 Nottingham Way, Hillside, N.J. 1972.

Hass, Hans, THE HUMAN ANIMAL, N.Y. Putnam's Sons. 1970.

Holt, Emmett, Jr. CARE AND FEEDING OF CHILDREN, N.Y. Appleton-Century. 1943.

Homan, William, CHILD SENSE, N.Y. Basic Books, Inc. 1969.

Hormann, Elizabeth, RELACTATION: A GUIDE TO BREASTFEEDING THE ADOPTED BABY, 1 Merril Ave., Belmont, Mass. 1971.

Hymes, James, CHILD UNDER SIX, Englewood Cliffs, N.Y. Prentice Hall, Inc. 1963.

Janov, Arthur, THE PRIMAL SCREAM, N.Y. Dell Publ. 1970.

Janov, Arthur, THE FEELING CHILD, N.Y. Simon and Schuster. 1973.

Josselyn, Irene, PSYCHOSOCIAL DEVELOPMENT OF CHILDREN, Family Service Assoc. of America, N.Y. 1948.

Kippley, Sheila, BREASTFEEDING AND NATURAL CHILD SPACING, N.Y. Harper and Row. 1974.

Kippley, John and Sheila, THE ART OF NATURAL FAMILY PLANNING, P.O. Box 11084, Cincinnati, Ohio 45211.

La Leche League of Minnesota Third State Seminar Transcripts, April, 1972, 9616 Minneapolis Avenue, Franklin Park, Ill. 60131.

La Leche League International reprints, LLLI, 9616 Minneapolis Ave., Franklin Park, Ill. 60131.

La Leche League Third Biennial Convention Transcript, LLLI, Franklin Park, Ill. 60131. 1968.

La Leche League Manual, THE WOMANLY ART OF BREASTFEEDING, LLLI, Franklin Park, Ill. 60131. 1958.

Langer, Lawrence, "The Pursuit of Happiness," an American Comedy. N.Y. Samuel French. 1934.

Lerich, Constance, MATERNITY NURSING. St. Louis, Mosby Co. 1970.

Lindgren, H. and Byrne, D. PSYCHOLOGY, N.Y. Wiley and Sons, Inc. 1971.

Lorenz, Konrad, KING SOLOMON'S RING, N.Y. Crowell Comp. 1952.

Luce, Gay and Segal, Julius, SLEEP, N.Y. Coward-McGann, 1966.

Luce, Gay and Segal, Julius, INSOMNIA, Garden City, N.Y., Doubleday and Comp. 1969.

Marlow, Dorothy, TEXTBOOK OF PEDIATRIC NURSING, Philadelphia, Saunders Com. 1969.

Mead, Margaret, FROM THE SOUTH SEAS, N.Y. Morrow, 1939.

Moloney, James, FEAR: Contagion and Conquest, Philosophical Library, N.Y. 1957.

Montagu, Ashley, MAN: HIS FIRST MILLION YEARS, N.Y. Mentor Book. 1957.

Montagu, Ashley, TOUCHING: The Human Significance of the Skin, N.Y. Columbia Univ. Press. 1971.

Montagu, Ashley, ON BEING HUMAN, N.Y. Hawthorn Book, Inc. 1966.

Montagu, Ashley, THE NATURAL SUPERIORITY OF WOMEN, N.Y., McMillan Comp. 1968.

Montessori, Maria, THE SECRETS OF CHILDHOOD, N.Y. Frederick Sotkes, 1939.

Montessori, Maria, THE ABSORBENT MIND, N.Y. Holt, Rinehart, and Winston, 1973.

Morris, Desmond, INTIMATE BEHAVIOR, N.Y. Random House. 1971.

Neill, A. S., SUMMERHILL, N.Y. Hart Publ. Comp. 1959.

Newton, Niles and Hoeber, Paul, MATERNAL EMOTIONS, N.Y. Medical Book Depart. of Harper and Row, 1955.

Newton, Niles, FAMILY BOOK OF CHILD CARE, N.Y. Harper and Row. 1957.

Nichols, J. L., SAFE COUNSEL, Chicago, Ill, Franklin Publ. 1928.

Packard, Vance, THE SEXUAL WILDERNESS, N.Y. David McKay Comp. 1968.

Pryor, Karen, NURSING YOUR BABY. N.Y. Pocket Books, 1973.

Richardson, S. A. et al, CHILDBEARING: ITS SOCIAL AND PSYCHOLOGICAL ASPECTS, Williams and Wilkens. 1967.

Ribble, Margaret, THE RIGHTS OF INFANTS, N.Y. Columbia Univ. Press. 1965.

Salk, Lee and Kramer, Rita, HOW TO RAISE A HUMAN BEING. N.Y., Random House. 1969.

Salk, Lee, WHAT EVERY CHILD WOULD LIKE HIS PARENTS TO KNOW. N.Y. McKay Comp. 1972.

Spock, Benjamin, BABY AND CHILD CARE. N.Y. Pocket Books. 1968.

Stiles, Henry Reed, BUNDLING: Its Origin, Progress and Decline in America, Albany, Knickerbocker Publ. 1871.

Thomas, Elizabeth, THE HARMLESS PEOPLE, N.Y., Knopf, 1959.

Ziegel, Erna and v. Blarcom, Carolyn, OBSTETRIC NURSING, N.Y. McMillan Comp. 1972.

Magazines

BIRTH AND FAMILY JOURNAL, Vol. 1, No. 3, 1974, Klaus, Marshall, editorial, 110 El Camino Real, Berkeley, Ca. 94705.

CEAN TODAY, Newsletter of CEA of Minneapolis and St. Paul, P. O. Box 20091, Minneapolis, Minn. 55420, Aug. 1973. "Ear Infections."

CHILD AND FAMILY Quarterly, ed. Vol. 19, No. 4, 1960, Ed. Herbert Ratner, M.D., P.O. Box 508, Oak Park, Ill. p. 2

CHILD AND FAMILY DIGEST, Vol. 9, No. 3, P.O. Box 508, Oak Park, Ill. 1970.

ETHNOLOGY, Vol. 10, Barry, M. III, Paxson, L. M., "Infancy and Early Childhood: Cross-Cultural Codes 2," Oct. 1971.

HARVARD EDUCATIONAL REVIEW, Ryerson, Alice, "Medical Advice on Childrearing 1550-1900," Vol. 31, No. 3, p. 302.

HOUSE AND GARDEN, Russel, "To Share or Not to Share," May, 1971. p. 98.

MARRIAGE, Kenny and Schreiter, "Of Babies, Beds and Teddy Bears," Jan. 1971.

NATIONAL FOUNDATION OF SUDDEN INFANT DEATH Pamphlet, "Facts About Sudden Infant Death Syndrome," 1501 Broadway, N.Y. 10036. 1970.

NATIONAL GEOGRAPHIC, 1972. p. 244.

NEW SOCIETY, "Why Some Babies Don't Sleep," Bernal, Richard , Feb. 28, 1974, England.

NEWSWEEK, "What Is a Mother to Do?" Sept. 23, 1968.

OBSTETRICAL SOCIETY OF LONDON, Martyh, W., "On the Management of Childbed," 1870. p. 339.

PARENTS' MAG. Arnstein, Helene, "How Babies Learn to Wait," Dec. 1970.

PARENTS' MAG. Whipple, Dorothy, "The Magic of Sleep," May, 1967.

PARENTS' MAG. Johnston, M. "Discipline or Indulgence?" July, 1969.

PSYCHIATRY, Montagu, Ashley, "Some Factors in Family Cohesion," Vol. 7, 1944.

PSYCHOLOGY TODAY, Newton, Niles, "Breastfeeding," Jn. 1968.

PSYCHOLOGY TODAY, Breetveld, James, "Mother and Child in Africa," Feb. 1972. p. 63.

PSYCHOLOGY TODAY, Krebs, R., "Interruptus," Jan. 1970. p. 153.

READERS' DIGEST, Ratcliff, J.D., "I'm Joe's Skin," June, 1972.

REDBOOK, Brecher, R., "Why Some Mothers Reject Their Babies," May 1966. p. 49.

SCRIBER'S MAGAZINE, 1893.

SCIENTIFIC DIGEST ED. Report on Sleep Research, June 1971. p. 57.

SCIENTIFIC AMERICAN, Salk, Lee, "Role of the Heartbeat in the Relationship Between Mother and Infant," May 1973.

TODAY'S HEALTH MAG., Cox, James, "When Bedtime Brings Problems," May, 1967.

U.S. DEPARTMENT OF HEALTH, EDUCATION AND WELFARE, Washington, D.C., "Infant Care" 1967.

ORDER FORM

Remit this form, or copy the information on a card and send to:

> Tine Thevenin
> P.O. Box 16004
> Minneapolis, MN
> 55416

Price per book is $4.95. (Price is subject to change.)

Please send me _____ number of copies of THE FAMILY BED:
    AN AGE OLD CONCEPT IN CHILDREARING,

@ $4.95 . . . . $ _____ . ___

Postage and handling, first book . . . . $ _____ . 75

Add 30 cents for each additional book . . . . $ _____ . ___

Minnesota residents add 4% sales tax . . . . . $ _____ . ___

Enclosed is my check for: Total $ _____ . ___

(Please send no c.o.d.'s or cash.)

(Please print clearly.)

Name _____

Street _____

City _____ State _____ Zip _____